Planting with Prayer

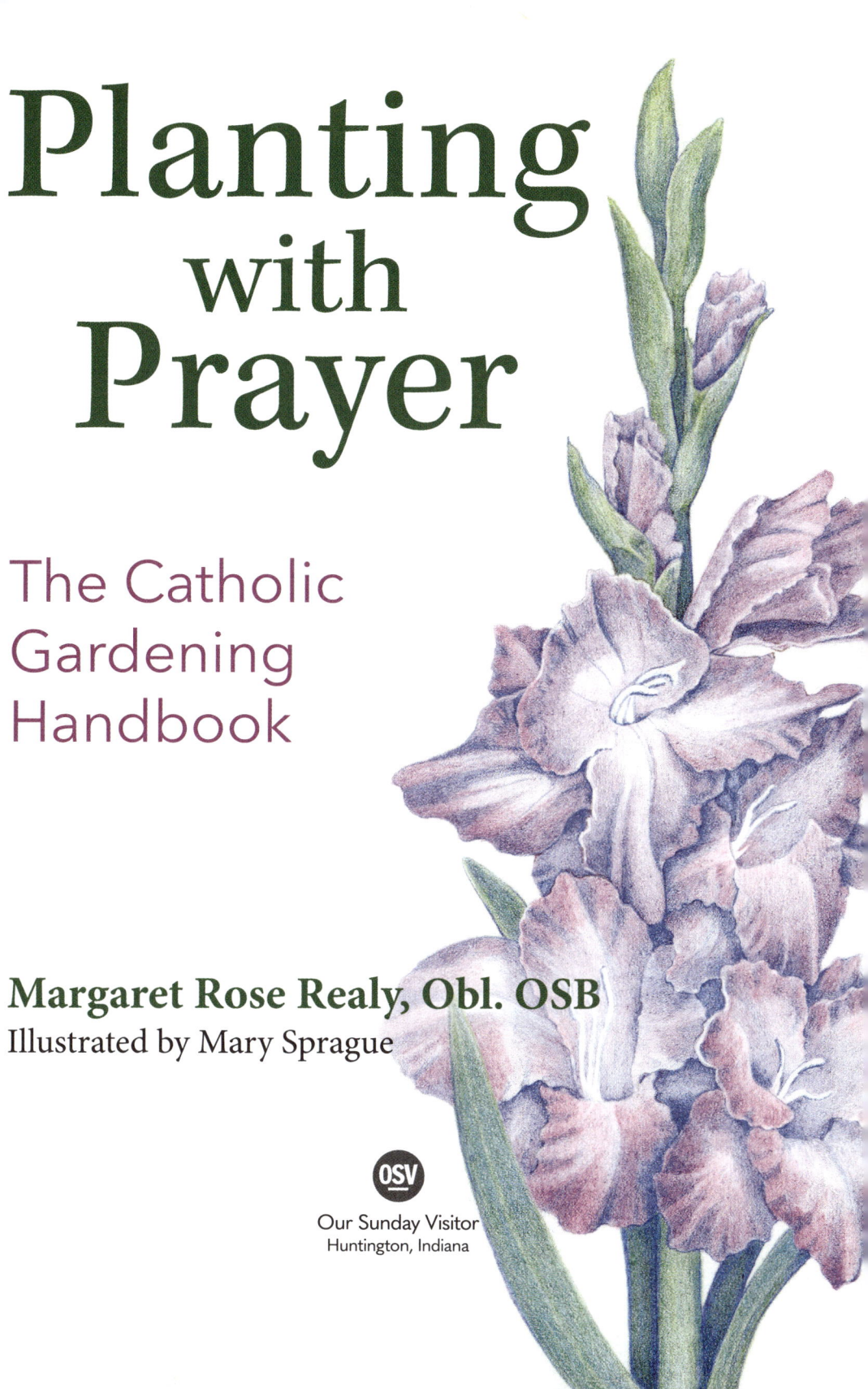

Planting with Prayer

The Catholic Gardening Handbook

Margaret Rose Realy, Obl. OSB
Illustrated by Mary Sprague

OSV
Our Sunday Visitor
Huntington, Indiana

Nihil Obstat
Msgr. Michael Heintz, Ph.D.
Censor Librorum

Imprimatur
✠ Kevin C. Rhoades
Bishop of Fort Wayne-South Bend
August 13, 2024

The *Nihil Obstat* and *Imprimatur* are official declarations that a book is free from doctrinal or moral error. It is not implied that those who have granted the Nihil Obstat and Imprimatur agree with the contents, opinions, or statements expressed.

Excerpts from the *Revised Standard Version of the Bible* — Second Catholic Edition (Ignatius Edition) Copyright © 2006 National Council of the Churches of Christ in the United States of America. Used by permission. All rights reserved worldwide.

Excerpts from the English translation of the *Catechism of the Catholic Church* for use in the United States of America Copyright © 1994, United States Catholic Conference, Inc. — Libreria Editrice Vaticana. Used with Permission. English translation of *the Catechism of the Catholic Church*: Modifications from the Editio Typica copyright © 1997, United States Conference of Catholic Bishops—Libreria Editrice Vaticana.

Every reasonable effort has been made to determine copyright holders of excerpted materials and to secure permissions as needed. If any copyrighted materials have been inadvertently used in this work without proper credit being given in one form or another, please notify Our Sunday Visitor in writing so that future printings of this work may be corrected accordingly.

Copyright © 2025 by Margaret Rose Realy
30 29 28 27 26 25   1 2 3 4 5 6 7 8 9

All rights reserved. With the exception of short excerpts for critical reviews, no part of this work may be reproduced or transmitted in any form or by any means whatsoever without permission from the publisher. For more information, visit: www.osv.com/permissions.

Our Sunday Visitor Publishing Division
Our Sunday Visitor, Inc.
200 Noll Plaza
Huntington, IN 46750
www.osv.com
1-800-348-2440

ISBN: 978-1-63966-223-4 (Inventory No. T2910)
1. GARDENING—General.
2. REFERENCE—Personal & Practical Guides.
3. RELIGION—Christianity—Catholic.

eISBN: 978-1-63966-223-4
LCCN: 2024948130

Cover and interior design: Amanda Falk
Cover and interior art: Mary Sprague

PRINTED IN THE UNITED STATES OF AMERICA

O most honored Greening Force,
You who roots in the Sun;
You who lights up, in shining serenity, within a wheel
that earthly excellence fails to comprehend.
You are enfolded
in the weaving of divine mysteries.
You redden like the dawn
and you burn: flame of the Sun.

— *Hildegard von Bingen,* Causae et Curae

Contents

Foreword	9
Author's Note	13
Introduction	15

Part 1 — Creating a Prayer or Memorial Garden

Unit 1 — Discern

1	Gathering Supplies	21
2	Defining the Garden	23
3	Memorial Gardens	33
4	Collecting Ideas	37

Unit 2 — Design

5	Prayer Garden Location	45
6	Site Assessment	49
7	Our Senses	59
8	Basic Building Blocks of Design	69
9	Hardscape	77
10	Plant Selection	81
11	Container Gardens	91
12	Drawing It All Out	97

Unit 3 — Develop

13	Preparation and Installation	103
14	Gardening Tools	109
15	Gardening Techniques	113
16	Composting	121
17	Fertilizer	123

Part 2 — Continuing to Grow

18	Prayer Garden Journaling	129
19	Tracking Sunlight and Shade	199
20	Soil Amendments	203
21	Watering Needs/Schedule	207
22	Tracking Diseases, Pests, and Weeds	211
23	Compost Rotation Chart	215
24	Plant Selection and History	219
25	Wish List	241

About the Author	245
Create Your Own Index	247

Foreword

Margaret Rose Realy is a teeny-tiny woman who loves truth and beauty. Being one of those people for whom creation inspires and draws forth even more creativity, she assists the Creator through her work, actively supplementing the abundant beauty of the world through her garden designs, her writing, and the scenic or faith-filled images she paints in her little hermitage-cum-studio.

In her quiet way, Margaret thus brings life to places made dead by shadowy darkness, particularly those shades that are the result of permanent, perspective-scarring installations we can neither ignore nor tear down on our own, because their erections have been permitted. Through her passions and her eagerness to discern the call of her Master, she brings oxygen into places that can seem smothering, brightens a dreary corner, or soothes what is whirling by offering words or places of lasting stillness.

In case you're wondering, yes, my meaning here is both actual and metaphorical. All of us know what it is to live with dark shadows of memory and spirit that we never wanted or anticipated, and it can take decades — or even a whole lifetime, sometimes — to begin to understand why God has permitted them. We all have found ourselves suffocating at some point from feelings of guilt or shame or the simple confusion of wondering how we got where we are. The work that Margaret Rose Realy does in her gardens — the work she is encouraging us to take on and internalize and grow from with this book and her other works — can help us to become proficient in cooperating with the light we enjoy as we learn to do our best possible with the stubbornly intrusive shadows we must endure.

This is her gift, and she shares it with endless passion, expertise, and attention to detail, encouraging readers to journal through unavoidable points of discovery. Hey, there are worse ways to recognize your own emotional or spiritual state than by studying dirt sediments!

Expect unexpected insights here. For instance, Margaret's suggestion that 10 percent of a garden should boast white flowers in order to help the rest "pop" was a revelation to me — one that translated into including hourly, one-sentence prayer interludes into my day, supplying a burst of brightness to my own interior life.

Speaking of prayer, the other thing you should know about Margaret is that she is a Benedictine oblate who — like the great Benedictine polymath and Doctor of the Church, St. Hildegard of Bingen — does many things well, but nothing that is not rooted in prayer. She is, in fact, a prayer warrior. Each week on her Facebook page, she invites your attention with a glorious image and then asks, "How may I pray for you this week?"

Her request is not grandiose, but rather a humble request to serve others — which Margaret views as a privilege — through the subversive and infinite power of contemplative and intercessory prayer. As someone who has benefited from those prayers, I know that she takes on the requests and needs of others with genuine gladness and the confident heart of a hermit running to the Beloved One in whom she trusts. She reminds me of the psalmist, who wrote, "For the sake of the house of the Lord our God, I will seek your good" (Ps 122:9).

Through this gentle, encouraging book we can discover how everything we learn in a garden, as we wrangle earth, air, water, and the fiery sun can be extrapolated into the spiritual realm, where we wrangle emotions, tensions, hopes, and fears, and that can be a little intimidating. Like the angels, Margaret encourages us to "be not afraid," and sends us off with a warm prayer.

    I would only add that we plant boldly; boldness in planting signals a boldness of trust.

Elizabeth Scalia
Montauk, NY
June 29, 2024

Author's Note

The great twelfth-century mystic, healer, and philosopher, St. Hildegard von Bingen, created the word *veriditas*, Latin for *das Grün*, or "the green." This "greening of the mind" — the growth of intelligence and spiritual insight through encountering and understanding nature — describes Hildegard's vision of the power of nature to connect us with knowledge of God through creation. It is her expression of the synergistic concept in Christian Tradition which combines nature's manifest vitality and mankind's encounter with God.

God seems always close and speaks clearly to my heart whenever I seek him in a garden. I have always been involved with gardening and growing. Our family business was greenhousing; my maternal grandmother and I would garden together whenever we could; and I started college with botany and horticulture, though I graduated with a business degree.

Many years later, when the economy plummeted and employment became scarce for a woman in her fifties, I sought the peace of gardening and growing once more. I had already completed the requirements to be an Advanced Master Gardener, so I studied and received certification as a greenhouse grower and began working in the green industry. As a landscape consultant, I helped many customers with questions and realized how hungry others were for the solace that could be found in a garden.

This sparked a growing awareness: I wanted to combine my desire to serve God with this talent he had given me. I began creating prayer gardens on the ninety-five acres of St. Francis Retreat Center in DeWitt, Michigan.

As I worked, I prayed that others would find a way to come to the gardens — that if they could silence the din of daily life enough, they might begin to hear God's gentle voice. I felt assured that the Holy Spirit would do the rest and bring them peace. As I planted and weeded at church gardens and at the retreat center, the visitors I saw were testimony that my prayers were being answered.

After presenting several workshops and creating numerous handouts for participants, I wrote my first book, *A Garden of Visible Prayer: Creating a Personal Sacred Space One Step at a Time*. It was first accepted for publishing by Circle Media in 2007, later printed by Faith Publishing in 2011, and reprinted again by Patheos Press in 2014. The book remained popular and on the market until 2022 — astonishing to all but the Holy Spirit. The encouragement of those who found the peace of God in those simple gardens, and others who wanted to know how to create their own sacred spaces, led to small gatherings to discuss the book. Later, I guided retreats where attendees began the process of connecting spiritually to creating visible prayer through a garden setting.

Thanks to OSV, that little instructive book is revised and expanded upon in these pages. *Planting with Prayer* follows *A Garden Catechism: 100 Plants in the Christian Tradition and How to Grow Them* (OSV, 2022), though each book stands on its own. Readers of *A Garden Catechism* may be familiar with some of the matter presented here, and will appreciate the expanded section that includes traditional garden journal worksheets, and prayer journaling pages. New readers — including those brand-new to gardening — will find in this book all they need to design and maintain a prayer garden, and can turn to *A Garden Catechism* for a deeper dive into specific plants and their symbolism.

Introduction

God transforms the depths that define the surface.[*]

As an industrial and technological society, we are losing sight of what brings us solace and also losing our memory of what is sacred. We are losing ourselves in the daily demands of job and family commitments and in the upkeep of our homes. More importantly, we are losing our ability to connect with God through the physical world he created for us. It is increasingly difficult to find a place of inner peace, that quiet place within our souls that allows us to rest in God, converse with him, and contemplate his goodness. In this quiet place we can find spiritual joy, strength, and the energy to continue. We hunger to return to our place of origin, back to the garden where Adam and Eve walked with God.

This book is a step-by-step approach to help guide you in creating and maintaining a meaningful sacred space — a place close at hand that you can easily step into, and that brings you, in all your individuality, to inner quietness.

When working with people who want to create a prayer garden, I

---

[*] *Magnificat*, Oct. 2019, vol. 21, no. 8, 319.

often find that they don't even know how to define what it is they seek or where to begin. Some individuals surrender to the lack of direction by plopping a bench down in the corner of their yard, setting a container of annuals next to it, and calling it good enough. Others spend a lot of money and long hours developing a garden only to find that, though beautiful by definition, their created landscape doesn't touch their spirit as they had hoped it would. People can end up with a random selection of elements they like, but a lack of spiritual cohesion brings little more than "Meh."

God created each one of us unique, and as a result, each of us relates to the natural world in our own way.

So, the first step is to identify what moves *you* in this season of your life and spiritual growth. This is the time to look beyond your grandmother's garden or your neighbor's orderly plantings. You may find that, much like decorating your home, a single item inspires you or brings a warm memory. Just as you may have a way of prayer that works for you, a particular color, shape, or even texture may, in your garden, reflect that. Considering plants that get you saying, "I like that" will help identify what can be spiritually significant for you.

In her book *Spiritual Gardening*, Peg Streep emphasizes the importance of "[tending to your] inner landscapes and foster[ing] the growth of your spirit."* In quieting ourselves, the seed of God can enter into the fertile soil of our soul and lead us to bear the fruit he has purposely planted within us.

Many inspiring books can help you in understanding the elements of landscape design and how certain aspects of a landscape affect us. This book does not consider whole-yard projects, but only the very small portion of your living space that can best help you attend to the landscape of your soul.

As we begin a step-by-step process of creating a personalized garden of visible prayer, I pray that this book will help you create personal (or public) spaces for outdoor prayer. May the journey bring you closer to God, for it is in our very desire to find and please God that we indeed do so.

---

* Peg Streep, *Spiritual Gardening: Creating Sacred Space Outdoors* (Inner Ocean, 2003), 11.

PART 1
Creating a Prayer or Memorial Garden

UNIT 1
DISCERN

1
Gathering Supplies

This first step, the initial process of discerning your garden, will require you to assemble a few items for a garden creation notebook. Working through this process is meant to be a physical endeavor, literally a hands-on experience. You may find electronic devices to be of minimal use in this creative experience, and I encourage you to step away from gadgetry and engage in the process at a different level.

As you move through this book, you can title each tab in your binder according to the chapters. Not all chapters will be applicable to your individual needs. Remember, this is *your* notebook and it is filled with information that leads *you* to create the prayer garden that *you* desire. Later chapters will help you cull and refine your collected ideas.

ESSENTIAL SUPPLIES
- three-ring binder
- tabbed dividers
- a few pocket page protectors
- notebook paper, both lined and unlined
- tracing paper
- graph paper

- crayons, colored pencils, or pens
- lead pencils (with erasers!)
- a few white address labels
- scissors
- glue stick

NICE TO HAVE
- ruler
- circle templates
- a few sheets of assorted construction or scrapbooking paper (origami paper will work too)

2
Defining the Garden

Like the host waiting for us at the front of the Communion line, or the small light above the confessional, we know where to find Our Lord (Anonymous). So too do we know to seek him in his creation.

When we say something is sacred, we mean that it is consecrated to God in some way, dedicated or intentionally set aside for worship or prayer. Likewise, a sanctuary — most properly the place within our churches where the Sacrifice of the Mass is held — also refers to any place of refuge or protection. In a broader sense, we can set aside a personal space as sacred, as a sanctuary or haven where we return for prayer and spiritual refuge.

When we talk about connecting with God in prayer, or spiritual growth, what do we mean? Prayer is conversation with God, and a prayer garden is a place where we're able to focus and be present to that conversation. We're not just talking about a vague "spiritual connection"; we're talking about prayer. And we're not talking about vague "spiritual growth," but specifically growth in holiness, which is becoming more of who we were made to be.

Spiritually dedicated gardens are those that attend to the interior need of our soul, heart, and mind. We are both body and soul and are made to flourish in both. The beauty and peace of a garden supports our whole self: body, mind, and soul. Gardens are a place where both plants and people can grow. We find all of our senses engaged in a garden, and by creating a sacred space, we allow our spirit to grow in such a way that our interior landscape can reveal hidden hope.

Various types of gardens serve to help us flourish, either as individuals or in community. While most of us are looking to create a personal prayer garden, this book is also helpful for those creating a communal space.

Therapeutic gardens can contribute to a rehabilitation process that supports both mental and physical healing. A horticultural therapist may use a garden of this type to address a medical concern — perhaps helping a patient to recover lost skills — or to incorporate any sort of recovery regimen. Most therapeutic gardens are part of a medical or rehabilitation facility with restricted access.

Healing gardens are very similar to therapeutic gardens, with one key difference: The visitor to such a garden is not actively working with the physical environment. Healing gardens are more of an outdoor contemplative space. They are designed to lower physical and emotional stress and assist in personal renewal. This type of garden nurtures the spirit while the body is healing. Many healing gardens are part of a medical or care facility, and are usually public spaces, but they can be private gardens. Some herbal-centered medicinal or aromatherapy gardens are also called healing gardens.

Meditative or prayer gardens are specifically meant for prayer, discernment, and renewal. A garden of this nature may reflect the religion or philosophical belief system of the designer or visitors, and may not always be based in Christianity. Designs of these gardens will very often include sacramental elements and symbolic plants. Meditative prayer gardens can be either public or private spaces.

Memorial gardens are garden spaces specifically constructed to reflect or honor an individual, group, or topic. Memorial gardens are meditative simply by their very purpose in focusing our attention on a particular subject. Again, these gardens can be both public and private spaces. Chapter 3 is dedicated to creating this type of garden.

As you can see from these definitions, garden types easily overlap. Many of the concepts and most of the procedures addressed in this book can be applied to both public and private gardens. The type of garden you intend to create is loosely defined by how you intend to use it.

When conceptualizing your space, keep in mind whether it is to be a public garden being created for an organization or a private space for you or your family and friends. Your private garden will reflect what brings you, personally, to closeness with God. A public garden will be created for others, focusing on their desires, their possible needs, and how they will use the space. When creating a public garden, you should adhere to city and state codes, so do your homework and learn what these are before starting the installation.

DEVELOPMENT OF INTENT

A series of several questions will help you focus and will put you in the best frame of mind for planning your prayer garden. Although these may seem simplistic and obvious, answer them nonetheless. Open yourself up in prayer as you answer these questions and write down your answers; this is the start of your garden creation notebook. At the end of this section, you'll find additional space to write and reflect with these questions.

- What are the reasons you visit a garden? Is it because you find it calming, because you appreciate its aesthetic beauty, because you like sharing time with others or God, or because you want to reenergize yourself?
- Why do you want to create a sacred space? Is it to find peace, to escape from the din of daily life, or to experience solitude?
- Who is the subject of this garden? Is it for you? Is it a public space? Is it for someone who is deceased?
- How will it be used? Is it to be a memorial, a retreat, or a place to meditate?
- How will it function (such as, a public space for baptisms, an

extended sanctuary of a church, a place for outdoor worship, etc.)?
- How will you or others occupy this space? Will you sit in it most of the time? Will you walk within it? Will you use it in the morning or at the gloaming of the day? Will you welcome others into it?
- Where will it be located? Behind the garage, under a stand of pines, or in the vacant lot next to the church?

Really consider your answers. Do you see a pattern of intent or purpose? Synonymous words should be present in your answers; circle them, rewrite them, and pray over them. These intentions are your foundation.

THE LOOK OF SPIRITUALITY

Here you will identify what objects help put you in a prayerful frame of mind. In other words, what aspects of a garden induce a sense of spirituality for you? Many years ago, I attended a program about the history and creation of a spiritual landscape* and came away with many insights and one tool I still use — a form that I have adapted and include here. You should begin with this form too, and here is how to prepare it.

1. Take a sheet of paper and divide it into three columns. Write these headings across the top of the three columns:

Items	Adjectives	Emotions

2. Beginning in the Items column, list the elements you would likely find in a garden. Things like water, birds, rocks, yellow flowers, blue gazing ball ... Just write down whatever comes to mind.

3. In the next column, Adjectives, write down characteristics or descriptions of each item you included in the first column. An example would be *rock — solid, still, unmoving; blue gazing ball — reflective, fragile*. Take your time to really think about which words describe the items in the first column.

---
* Dr. Frank Dunbar, "Designing a Spiritual Landscape" (Hidden Lake Gardens, Tipton, MI, July 9, 2005).

4. The last aspect to consider is what emotions are evoked by these items. This column takes a little more time, as well it should. Here you are identifying what feelings you want to nurture in your sacred space. Using the example of *rock — solid, still, unmoving* could evoke positive emotions of being *strong, dependable*, or negative ones of being *cold* and *hard*. These emotions will be different for each person. For example, I personally like large boulders in a garden, yet some of my clients have a real aversion to what they would describe as a hunk of stone lying around.

Remember that there is absolutely no right or wrong response in your list. No matter what you write in the last column, the answer will be correct, so be honest with yourself. It will do you no good to try to please someone else with your answers. For example, a vivid orange flower might be beautiful to one person, but you really dislike that color. Or, if you are allergic to oranges, your true response would be a negative one.

Sample Table

Items	Adjectives	Emotions
Rock	Solid, still, unmoving	Strong, secure
Blue gazing ball	Fragile, reflective	Contemplation
Tall grasses	Flowing, rapid growth, movement	Openness

Fragrance is a topic that deserves attention. In your table, draw a horizontal line under what you have previously written or start a new set of columns. You will add a new section and it will be called "Scents." In the Items column here, list the scents you like and the ones that stir your memory, and how they are evoked. Examples are *lilies by air movement, lavender by touch, alyssum by heat/air*, and so on.

The Adjectives column is often more difficult to fill in with scents because the other senses are not involved. Describing the characteristic of a fragrance is challenging to all but the most gifted of poets. Scent is personal and very subjective. For example, the Oriental lily Stargazer can be described as both heavy and dizzying.

Because fragrances or aromas have a more powerful and direct psychological effect than the other senses, filling in the Emotions column is much easier.

Remember also to identify those scents that are not your favorites when considering a fragrance in your garden. A dear friend of mine develops severe headaches at the scent of spring hyacinths (*Hyacinthus orientalis*). Another woman finds that the scent of paperwhite narcissus reminds her of her cat's litter box!

What negative associations, if any, do you have to certain fragrances? Make note of them in your table as well. Add the plant with a negative association in the Items column and include in the Emotions column a red X. You will want to avoid inadvertently adding those scents of a symbolic plant as your design progresses.

The last portion of your table is about colors. There is a section in chapter 7 dedicated to this aspect, but for now, our purpose is to identify the emotions that certain colors evoke. Again, draw another horizontal line to start a new set of columns labeled Colors, and fill in each column accordingly as you work across the chart.

If as a child you had Crayola Crayons™ you may remember that the colors were labeled in very creative ways — Carnation Coral, Aztec Gold, Jungle Green. Each one inspired a response and often made me smile. Remember that in a garden, green is more than the background. It too is a color and there are a lot of shades of green to be considered. The subtleties of color will help you discover what inspires your spirit.

FOCUSING YOUR INSPIRATIONS

This concluding step will help narrow your vision on what you need as well as what you want in your garden. Look closely at your tables, especially the Emotions column, and circle the responses that point you in the direction of your desired outcome for a prayer space.

Even though when you look at the Emotions column you see a lot of feelings, circle only those that best fit the intent of your space as designated in the first part of this chapter. If you intend to use your space to invigorate your life, words like "moving" or "delight" should be circled. Should your space be designed as a quiet retreat, then your designated words would be "calming" or "reflective."

Travel from right to left in your table, from the Emotions that you have circled to the associated Items. Here are the basic building blocks for your space — highlight those items, then select one as the focal point of your meditative or prayer space. It could be a wrought-iron piece of art shaped like a cross, a colorful gazing ball, or a clump of 'Karley Rose' ornamental grass (*Pennisetum orientale* 'Karley Rose'). This meditative item will be the last element you will install in your garden.

You have now completed a crucial step in defining your sacred space. You have identified your intentions of how you will use it, what emotions you want to evoke, and what objects will fulfill those needs.

For many of us, the hardest part is now done. The following chapters are simply the plug-and-play of designing.

JOURNAL _____

Invite the Holy Spirit into your journaling, asking for guidance in prayerfully considering these questions:

What are the reasons you visit a garden?

Why do you want to create a sacred space?

Who or what is the subject of this garden?

How will it be used? What is its function?

How will you or others occupy this space?

Where will it be located?

3
Memorial Gardens

For happiness one needs security, but joy can spring like a flower even from the cliffs of despair.

— Anne Morrow Lindbergh

This is a very brief chapter with a very specific focus. Memorial gardens are garden spaces specifically constructed to reflect or honor an individual, group, or topic. They are meditative simply by their very purpose of focusing our attention on an individual or event. Catholic memorial gardens could include one for preborn babies whose death preceded birth or could be in honor of a saint, a holy person, a beloved parish priest, or a founder of a religious order.

There is a great deal more freedom in creating a personal memorial garden for, let's say, your sister, than there would be in creating a public space to honor soldiers or unborn children. Public spaces must be designed with the needs of others kept in mind, and according to the regulations of the municipality. You can still use the exercises in the previous chapter, but give added attention to which elements evoke appropriate responses associated with the intended memorial within the community where it is placed.

The key here is identifying the culture of the community who will be using the space. A memorial suited to the culture and style of a Middle Eastern Christian community — one that could include a water feature and regional flora — will be very different from one for a predominantly Polish neighborhood where icons and shrines could be included along a garden path. Remember, it is important to consult with the community you are working with to determine what such cultural reflections might include.

At this stage, be very open about potential images and concepts. Remember, you are constructing a notebook, so enter the written answers to the following questions into it; refining them will come later.

When designing a memorial or prayer garden for a community, the following questions should be answered:

1. What process is needed to create the garden? (This is a simple step-by-step project management plan working backwards from the completion date. It includes such things as permits, land grant titles, a materials acquisition list, and the dates these things are due for the project to continue in a timely manner.)
2. What elements should be included based on cultural association? For example, elements used for a Catholic Hispanic community (*milagro* hearts, Virgin of Guadalupe icon) are not the same as those you would use for Japanese Catholics (triptych shrine of Our Lady of China, chrysanthemums, plum trees).
3. What images and symbols will reflect the sacred for this identity group?
4. What site location will best fit the sacred space? (Be sure to consider exposure to sun and wind, the view from outsiders, and potential distractions, such as local noise patterns, local traffic patterns, or physical structures.)

5. When considering a person to be memorialized within a garden, or whether the space will be private or public, the questions are much the same:
6. Who is the memorial garden about: the person or the family?
7. What is it that he or she loved, or that he or she did? What was his or her favorite color, or most valued object?
8. What is it that you, your family, or a community loved about him or her?

Sometimes a memorial garden will include an artifact that is very special and specific to the person. If your brother was a firefighter, you may have a statue of a Dalmatian tucked in beside the red petunias. This is fine and very endearing in a private space. But such subtle references in a public space will detract from the overall essence and design of a memorial.

Take this information about the intent of the memorial garden and create a table as you did in chapter 2.

You may find it much easier to create your table when you are designing a memorial for a loved one, as you will already have a great deal of emotional information at the ready.

Whether you want to design a memorial garden or some other type, you will need to think about some essential components — that is what we will look at in the next chapter on collecting ideas.

JOURNAL

Pray with the Holy Spirit over your design choices for a community memorial garden.

How do you think the community would be affected by your design choices? How do these choices reflect the spirituality of the group?

What prayer might you wish to offer *in memoriam* when the garden — whether public or private — is formally dedicated?

4
Collecting Ideas

The garden affords a beautiful emblem of a Christian's continual progress in the path of virtue. Plants always mount upwards, and never stop in their growth till they have attained to that maturity which the Author of nature prescribed. So in a Christian, everything ought to carry him toward that perfection.

— Saint Serenus[*]

From your completed table, you now have a pretty good idea of what is reflective of your spirituality and will help you to move closer to God. Your table also reflects a recurring theme that, with a discerning heart, you have identified. Your garden design will begin here.

In this chapter we begin the process of making a wish list for your garden by collecting ideas and images. And you will probably collect a lot of them! Magazines and websites are your best tool — those that deal with the home, gardens, and travel are usually the most helpful.

---

[*] "St. Serenus, a Gardener, Martyr," TrueChristianity.Info. https://www.truechristianity.info/en/the_saints_02/saint_serenus_a_gardener_martyr.php.

The internet, especially Pinterest, is an amazing resource for images; some of them are not even set in gardens but help uncover how to convey an emotion. Unless you are good at narrowing your search, you could get lost in the results. I find that being fairly specific and scrolling through only the first three or so pages of results from an internet search prevents wasting time wandering around on the web.

The main purpose of seeking a collection of images for your garden's design is to help you to identify visually what you find pleasing. If you find an image that has a lot of interest to it but you only are drawn to one element, circle that element and/or post a note on the clipping, next to the feature, stating what drew you to it. Maybe it's the shape of a tree, or the line of a bench; whatever it is, make note. Otherwise, when you go back and look at your clippings you may have no idea why you saved that picture of a hillside in Quebec from *Travel and Leisure* magazine.

Remember the pocket page protectors I suggested in the list of supplies? Here is where you will use them. You will eventually mark the lower right-hand corner of each pocket with a white label that contains the heading of the essential or personal element you plan to incorporate into your garden. A list of essential elements and personal elements follows this section. You may not plan on using all of them, so only designate pockets for those elements that you like. Then place these pockets in your binder. (If you are relying on Pinterest or another site, label your boards and pins accordingly.)

As you clip or print out photos — a wonderful pastime in non-gardening months — place the images inside the appropriate pocket. In a surprisingly short time, as the collection grows, you will begin to see your preferences form a distinct style. Much as you discovered with your table, a careful study of your collection will show a theme begin to emerge.

You may be wondering why we are giving very little attention, right now, to the actual plants (and their symbolisms) which will actually grace your garden. Save all of your ideas, but the final plant selection process is a detailed activity we will discuss in chapters 6 and 10.

ESSENTIAL ELEMENTS
Transition Element
This is a crucial feature that designates the beginning or end of a garden. It cues you to alter your frame of mind because you are entering a different space. A transition element also can signify a sacred garden space within a larger garden. The element could include but is not limited to gates, arbors, and steps. Plantings can also indicate a transition, as can containers that are strategically placed. The term *transition* has other meanings in landscape architecture, but for our purpose here this definition will be sufficient.

Dividers
These are visual barriers that create a sense of enclosure in a prayer garden, like a row of tall grasses or a large container on a deck. Dividers are not for everybody. Some people may prefer a vista that is open to the eye and opens up the heart. Dividers can be part of the transition element or a stand-alone feature. They can be made of constructed materials or privacy plantings.

Seating
This can include benches, tables with chairs, or any arrangement you desire. Having a back to rest against is always nice if you intend to sit in your garden for a while. If you plan to share your space with others, be sure to include seating for them nearby. You may want to include a small table where you can write or set down a drink or book.

My personal preference is seating for two. This preference comes from a story told to me by a priest about one of his peers, who had gone to the house of a woman who was caring for her elderly and dying father. As the priest entered the bedroom to visit with the gentleman, the older man asked him to sit on the end of the bed instead of the chair that he was approaching.

The older man told the priest that the chair next to his bed was for Christ, whom he talked to from time to time. He asked that his daughter not be told, because she might think him addled and silly. So, through all his visits the priest sat on the edge of the bed and never mentioned it to her.

A short time later, the daughter called, very distraught. Her father had passed away and she had found him half fallen out of bed. She was grieved to think that her dad was trying to get up and she had not heard him. When he questioned the daughter at the wake, the priest learned that her father had his head and arms in the chair by his bed when she found him. At this, the priest shared with her what the old man had told him. The priest knew that her father had died resting his head in the lap of Christ, who sat in the chair next to his bed.

For me, not only in my room, but in my garden as well, there will always be a second chair.

Walkways

These can be as formal or as simple as you choose. In casual settings, they are best when curved, but if you like a formal garden space, then use straight lines. Be aware that straight lines and angles invigorate the senses because they create visual tension. As you collect images, the type of materials you like, such as stone, grass, or mulch, and the line you prefer for your walkway, will become clearer.

Shade

Sitting in the sun for an extended period of time can be uncomfortable and unhealthy. Unless you are planning a night garden as a sacred space, it will be important that you factor in a means for shade. One of the quickest ways to provide shade when none is available is with a divider trellis, strategically placed around seating on the side from which the sun comes. Another option is a hinged or cantilevered patio umbrella set in a base.

Water Feature

This element is probably the most often used as a focal point in any garden setting. It provides visual interest, sound, movement, and water for the fauna of the area. A water feature can be as simple as a shallow piece of ceramic tucked into the ground or as elaborate as a waterfall and pool. Keep your budget in mind as you cut out pictures. For now, maybe a fountain in the shape of a small urn will suffice until you can afford installing a reflective pond with koi.

Color

Our emotive and physical responses to color are as varied as there are hues. A section on color in chapter 7 will discuss colors in more detail. For now, focus on photos that coincide with the information revealed from the table you developed in chapter 2.

Generally speaking, calming tones are at the blue end of the spectrum, and invigorating colors are at the red/yellow end. Pastels are more soothing than richly saturated hues. Look for color in plants as well as in hardscape pieces (seating, containers, dividers, etc.).

Anchor Points

These are elements that draw attention. Anchor points are sometimes called focal points. They include things like art, sacramental items, water features, a vista, and so on. In landscape architectural terms, "Focal points are places that draw your eye, that cause you to focus for a moment during a visual sweep of a scene, that even orient you in that direction."* In a general sense, everything you clip out and save for your pockets has a point of interest, an item in it that drew your attention. Here, you want to collect images that will let you focus reflectively while in a small sacred space.

Habitat

This has to do with the fauna in your area: birds, deer, butterflies, or squirrels. Look for pictures of elements that will draw these creatures into (or away from) your space; things like a hummingbird water station, deer-deterrent fencing, and bird houses or feeders. You get the idea.

Plants

As you collect images of plants or illustrations of planting designs, keep in mind that these pictures will guide you in the final stage of plant selection. Remember that a landscape design consultant does not live at your house, and that few if any gardens really look like the magazine photo for more than a couple of hours.

---

* Janet Macunovich, *Designing Your Gardens and Landscapes: 12 Simple Steps for Successful Planning* (Storey, 2000), 28.

PERSONAL ELEMENTS

These are the parts of your sacred outdoor space not usually considered essential to a garden, but that reflect a singular element you may want included.

Memory Images

In chapter 3 on memorial gardens, I mentioned that items that were reflective or familiar to the individual could be used — sparingly — in a private garden, and very cautiously in a public space. Your collection of pictures will by its nature be specific to whom or what is being memorialized.

Verses and Quotations

These need to be very concise, easy to read, and appropriate to the theme of the space. One of my favorite activities in creating public prayer spaces is to imprint a short verse in the cement platform for seating by using a press-in cement lettering kit.

***

This chapter contains a lot of information about the things you want to include in your garden. Let yourself loose to collect an abundance of images to fill the pocket pages in your binder. You will find that a theme and a personal style emerge as you progress. In chapter 8 (unit 2) we will begin the process of culling them to best fit your desires for your prayer garden.

Collecting Ideas 43

JOURNAL

What item have you found that most immediately sparked a sense of spirituality?

What was it about the item that moved you closer to God?

How do the visually pleasing images that you've selected reflect your faith?

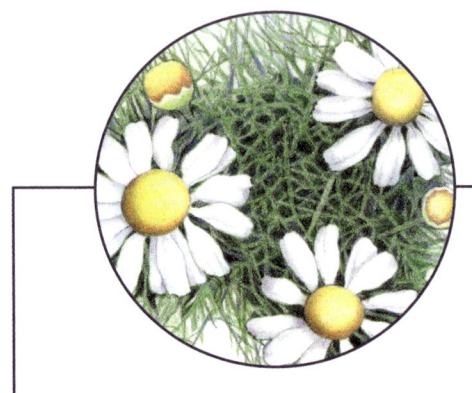

UNIT 2
DESIGN

5
Prayer Garden Location

In those moments … when everything is one, and when hand, heart, and habit reveal a body, mind, and spirit in full integration, centered and whole.

— Elizabeth Scalia[*]

If you have a very small yard, as I do, the location of your prayer space may already be evident and require only that you make the best of it. For those of you who have options, here are a few recommendations.

Your first consideration is when you will use the space and the orientation of the sun during that time. What hour of the day will you spend time in your private retreat? Will it be early mornings in preparation for heading out for the day? Mid-afternoon before the kids come home from school? After work? As mentioned before, it can be very uncomfortable and unhealthy to sit in the sun for an extended period of time, so plan to create shade if none exists during your preferred time.

---

[*] Elizabeth Scalia, "Making Ready for the Holy: 'A Man Will Meet You …,'" Word on Fire, April 12, 2022 https://www.wordonfire.org/articles/fellows/making-ready-for-the-holy-a-man-will-meet-you/.

If you plan to use your sacred space as a contemplative area, consider a quieter location away from distractions. If your focus is prayer and meditation about your family, have your house as the focal point from where you sit. If you will use your sacred space as a quick break in a busy day, make it easily accessible.

One of the most endearing and easily accessible prayer spaces I have ever encountered was created by a busy mom of meager means. She found a large rectangular trellis at a yard sale and attached it to the edge of the roof that hung over a cement slab porch. She hand-painted terra-cotta pots, in which she planted blue morning glories (*Ipomoea tricolor* 'Heavenly Blue') that grew up the trellis. She moved her small garden Madonna statue into this space and placed it on a matching inverted pot. Recycling some old brick, she created a spot for incense, and tossed down some old cushions that she had covered in tablecloths from the resale store. The sacred space was close at hand, quiet, reflected her faith, and incorporated those elements that led her to prayer.

Decks offer a variety of opportunities for prayer space. The deck area can be divided into rooms, much like the living spaces in a house. A corner of the deck will give more privacy than the center, and by using tall grasses in containers you can create a transition point or divider. Don't forget about the space beside the deck next to the house. This 90° corner has great potential because it offers a ready-made enclosed space nearby.

Other places that offer sheltered nooks are under or beside trees, by an existing trellis or arbor in your yard, or in spaces between the house and garage.

My first prayer garden made use of a narrow piece of lawn between the house and a six-foot stockade fence. After finally settling into the new house, and having done my homework all winter, I stepped out ready to create my garden early that first spring. I quickly completed this private little garden: narrow flower beds, shade from an old apple tree, cushioned chairs, a table made of small branches, and cement cherubs sitting on shelves created on the back of the fencing. Visually and spiritually pleasing, this prayer garden was small enough to evoke a sense of enclosure and to stimulate the senses. So don't hesitate to make that small side yard, the space behind the garage, or that shadowed corner next to the shed beautiful.

Although that first prayer garden seemed ideal, I would like to share my mistake in hopes of preventing someone else from making the same error. It became obvious as that first summer rolled around that I had not adequately anticipated the noise from the street — motorcycles and trucks with loud mufflers, motor homes rumbling along, and carloads of vacationers with blaring radios all made their way along the main road to the nearby resort lake. My very pretty garden was useless for contemplation.

As you look at different areas in your yard, imagine a line perpendicular to the side of the house, outbuilding, fence, or retaining wall. Drop an imagined line using these structures, a tree, or the side of a slope as a corner. Just imagine the possibilities for a private space — and now get a lawn chair.

Use the tried-and-true process of a lawn chair placed at different spots in your proposed location to determine where you will sit in your imagined garden space. Once you find a view or nook you like, leave the chair there for a few days. Look at the chair from inside the house. Does its location seem compatible with the view out your window? If you continue to gravitate to this spot when you're outdoors, you will have found your garden site.

Take a few photos of your lawn chair as it sits where your garden will be. Looking directly at the chair and standing a short distance away, take one picture each of the following: directly in front of the chair, standing behind it, and from each side. When it is time to draw your garden design, you will have a view from different angles to work with. Print and paste your pictures onto a sheet of notebook paper. On this same page write any observations and notes about your chosen location and add the sheet to your binder.

Also, look at your desired location during different times of the day and make notes. When is it in full sun? Does it stay damp too long in the morning or after a rain? Is that where the dog usually relieves itself? Note also what plants currently exist and, if they are suitable, how you can incorporate them into your design.

When you have decided where your garden will be located and some of its characteristics, it will be time to start assessing the site in the next chapter.

JOURNAL

When do you find prayer time most fruitful?

How will the location of your garden affect your prayer time?

6
Site Assessment

*A sacred space is a place for remembering not only
"who we are, but whose we are." It is a space where
seeds of quiet can enter in and grow Grace.**

Site assessment involves gathering information on the physical nature of your chosen garden area. There a few things to take into consideration after you have selected the location for your prayer space. As you work through each, make your final notes on the sheet that has the picture of your chair. We are working with a very small portion of your landscape, so your assessment will be narrow and focused.

Your site assessment will directly affect the plant selection for your garden, even before considering plant symbolisms. If you already have a garden in place and are only sectioning off a portion of it as a retreat area, then this chapter will simply provide you with an overview. Do make notes of your existing garden, for you may be inclined to adjust the plantings to match your new awareness of a sacred space or to add symbolic plants.

---
* Margaret Realy, *God in the Garden*, presentation, St. Francis Retreat Center, March 2006.

SUNLIGHT AND SHADE

You will want to know how many hours during the day direct sunlight rests on your location. Generally defined, full sun equals six or more hours, partial sun equals four to six hours, shade equals about two to four hours, and dense shade either receives no direct sunlight or only up to two hours.

Full sun	Part sun	Part shade	Dense full shade
6+ hours	4–6 hours	2–4 hours	>2 hrs

Use the journal page, Tracking Sunlight and Shade, in Part 2, to track the amount of sunlight on your garden location at different times during the day.

Notice the term *full sun*. This is unobstructed sunlight directly resting on a plant's leaves. Shade is altered or diffused sunlight. In your small garden you will probably have more than one kind of shade. An example would be a prayer space with a trellis divider next to where you sit, creating dappled shade, while at the same time there is a tree that blocks all sunlight at the end of your garden. Types of shade are defined as follows.

Dense Shade

No direct sunlight or two hours or less of it; includes heavy tree canopy and the north sides of buildings. Dense shade, as indicated above, completely blocks any rays of sun getting to the ground or only allows for a very brief period of sunlight. Many of you are familiar with walking in dense woodlands, or entering a tunnel-like space where branches intersect over a path. But dense shade can also describe that difficult section of yard between your house and your neighbor's garage. Another thing that may occur in this corridor-like space is that the only two hours of sunlight that do permeate the space could be mid- to late-afternoon, and this direct sunlight tends to burn the life right out of shade plants.

Full or Afternoon Shade
Six or more hours of solid shade. It includes the east side of a structure or high slope and is often referred to as "morning sun only." Morning sun is not as intense as that of mid-day or afternoon. A spot receiving morning sun followed by afternoon shade is preferred for plants that require partial shade.

Medium Shade
Four to six hours of shade and includes high shade. High shade allows bright, reflective sunlight into an area. This happens when tree branches are trimmed up high on the trunk and reflected light is available from things like siding, water, or cement. Plants often respond to this type of shade as though they were in light shade, even though direct sunlight is absent. A lot of times high shade and dappled are seen together.

Dappled or Light Shade
Three to four hours of shade is considered light shade. Dappled shade is sunlight between the leaves that moves throughout the day, as often seen on a lawn. Some sun-loving plants will survive but not thrive in this environment.

This may be a lot more information on shade than you wanted to know, but keep these terms in mind when your planting list begins to develop.

SOIL
For many home gardeners, this topic causes bewilderment. I will discuss some general terms very briefly and help you to quickly identify your soil type. There are many excellent reference books on the market and websites about soils and how to amend them, if you decide to expand your knowledge and gardening skills.

Start by looking around your site and seeing what plants grow and their overall conditions. Weeds are a very good indicator of soil type. Well-groomed lawns are not good indicators of soil conditions because they are often watered and fertilized instead of being self-supporting. Also look at the general condition of plants growing in the surrounding area and note which ones are thriving or spindly; look them up and learn what their growing conditions are. This will help you determine your own soil's condition.

Listed below are a few basic definitions of soil conditions.

Texture
This is determined by the relative portions of sand, silt, and clay. It is an inherent soil property of the area you live in. Texture influences the soil's properties such as drainage. With a little effort the texture of a small area of soil can be altered. You can improve the soil of a garden with amendments such as sphagnum moss, coir, and compost.

Tilth
The physical condition of the soil as it relates to ease of seeding, emergence, and root penetration. Essentially, this is the soil's ability to support plants. You can improve the tilth of soil by improving its texture.

Compaction
This means that the soil particles have been mechanically pressed together to the point of nearly eliminating the spaces for air and water movement. This creates a condition known as *hard pan*. Think of a dirt driveway — no amount of tilling will return this hard compacted soil to a cultivatable condition. It has lost its tilth.

SOIL STRUCTURE ANALYSIS
You can do a simple check of the soil at your site by digging a 6 in/15cm deep hole, which is the depth of most spades, picking up a handful of the soil, and lightly squeezing it. You are looking for the amount of moisture being retained. Obviously, if it has just rained, wait a couple of days for the soil to drain before doing this test.

When you squeeze the soil, is it really dry and crumbly (sandy)? Is it cool and slightly damp while holding together (loam)? Or is it heavy and somewhat gooey (clay)?

To further assess soil texture, a quick and well-known method uses a quart/liter jar, water, and soil. As the particles of soil separate, they will naturally sort themselves out by weight and will create layers: heavy sand will be at the bottom of the jar, medium-weight silt will be in the middle, and lighter clay will be at the top (although sometimes if clay is very fine and light it may float, making the water appear cloudy). The relative proportions of these layers help you see what type of soil you have.

Procedure for Soil Structure Analysis

1. Take a soil sample from a few 6 in/15cm deep holes dug at the site location. Remove debris, mix together, and break up any lumps. Then measure out one cup/one quarter liter of soil.
2. Get a quart/liter jar with a lid.
3. Put the soil in the bottom of the jar, fill the jar full of water to within ½ in/1.25 cm from the top, add only a couple of drops of dish soap, and screw on the lid — tightly.
4. Shake the living daylights out of the jar! Make sure all particles are thoroughly separated.
5. Set the jar aside in a location where it won't get bumped during the next twenty-four hours.
6. Get a ruler and hold it against the side of the jar. Begin measuring the sediments:
7. After one minute, measure and record the number of inches/ centimeters of the settled particles of sand.
8. After an hour, measure and record the depth of the soil, subtracting the level of sand recorded. This is silt.
9. After twenty-four hours, measure the level and subtract the two previous numbers. This is the clay.
10. Calculate the percentage: Divide the depth of each layer by the total depth of soil, and then multiply by one hundred.*

A relatively equal portion of sand and silt particles with a little clay is considered loam. This type, and sandy loam where you have a bit more sand than silt in your jar, are usually the best types for gardening. If you have a noticeable amount of clay, don't fret. There are plants that do well in clay, and other plants that are called "clay-busters."

---
* Taylor's Guide, *Gardening Techniques* (Houghton Mifflin Harcourt, 1991) 47–48.

A small caveat here: Just because your soil structure is hard and doesn't drain does not necessarily mean it is clay. Compacted soil that has lost its tilth has the same characteristics. Compacted soil will not separate out into three layers. In either situation — clay or compaction — planting a garden in that location is not your best option and you will need to give way to using containers.

We have discussed the soil's structure. To determine the chemical makeup of your soil, a soil sample will need to be analyzed. This can be done through your county's extension office, through landscape firms, or through any number of soil testing services. The soil analysis will tell you the pH level and percentages of other chemicals and trace elements present. This information will help you determine plant selection and possible fertilizing needs.

To keep track of this information, see the Soil Amendments chart in the worksheet section at the back of the book, chapter 21.

WATER SOURCE

A garden hose that can be dragged to your area is probably the most you will have to consider. If you have an in-ground watering system you may need to have the heads adjusted. Of course, if you plan on locating your prayer space at the back of forty acres, watering will be an issue.

Also be sure to consider how long the area remains wet or dry after a rain. The lack of water on a dry site will be a factor in how much time you will need to set aside to attend to the garden. If you have located your space in a sandy area, at the top of a slope, under the eaves of the house, or under a lot of surface-rooting trees such as *Acer*, you can be sure that the area will most likely be dry. To accommodate this type of soil in a small space, you could select drought-tolerant plants, amend the soil, use mulch to help hold more moisture, and plan to water regularly.

A yard that is in a low-lying area or one with a high water table would create drainage problems. If the area is damp, look where the downspouts are located if you are near a building. Can you reroute the downspouts, add a curved portion, or extend it? Obviously, a wet area is not an appropriate location for a garden if you plan to sit in it, although it may make a very nice rain garden (where water pools and the area remains damp) to look at.

EXPOSURE

In landscape architecture, this has more to do with heat and sun, wind, and frost. Though these are all factors to be considered in your garden as a whole, for our purposes we want to narrow the definition and look at how your site ensures that it will be a contemplative experience and will minimize distractions, both physically and mentally.

We have already mentioned how the sun and its heat are unhealthy and can make you uncomfortable in your prayer space. This exposure is easily managed with shade. If you do not have a tree or a building to provide shade, creating it can be easily accomplished. The simplest is a patio umbrella or a divider trellis. For a more dramatic look consider creating an awning-like structure of cloth called a *shade sail*.

For a full sun exposure on a deck you can use the umbrella or sail, or, if you can afford it, add a retractable awning. Installing a pergola or arbor to sit under will also give a sense of being in a room, and adding a bench-style swing provides a place to rock while praying.

Remember my story of my first privacy garden? It was very exposed to street noise. For your own garden, keep this in mind and the recreational activities that may take place nearby. A prayer garden on the other side of a garage that has a basketball hoop attached would not prove to be very relaxing if the kids are home.

Privacy and proximity to others is an important factor here. Do you want to be able to see others if they come into your yard or approach the side door? Would you rather feel that you are secluded? How private do you want your sacred space to be?

If you plan to use your space at night, be sure to consider intrusive light sources such as porch or flood lights and street lights. For safety while you walk around your garden consider small solar-powered stake lights. You may also want to plan for some low-level lighting for reading.

ROOTS

Some of us may be blessed to have shade trees in our yards. Their roots may prove challenging when creating a shade garden, but try to prevent damaging them too much when digging.

Where soil is lacking, lay ground cloth — not plastic! — over the exposed root knees and spread mulch around them to create a sitting area. Large containers are always a nice touch under shade trees. Adding an arbor or some type of divider around this space would create the sense of being in a small room.

As you are assessing your site, write down your observations and add them to your binder.

There are only a few more steps before beginning the design.

JOURNAL _____

Reflect on how some of the features in a garden reveal the nature of your soul.

Sunlight

Water

Shade

Exposure

Soil

Roots

7
Our Senses

The earth is intrinsically tied to our ability to delight in its goodness, to delight in its having been made by God.

— Norman Wirzba[*]

Our physical senses can help deepen our awareness of a garden and assist in leading us to meditation and prayer. Sounds, sight, fragrances and, to a lesser extent, touch, are all part of the garden experience.[†] As you read this chapter, make notes about how each sense can be personally experienced in your space.

SOUNDS, CREATED AND ORGANIC

Sounds take on a unique quality when we are being contemplative: the sounds of nature, the sounds of water, the sounds of a city, and the sounds of our family. We may desire to be receptive to some sounds in our prayer space. Other sounds we may want to minimize.

---

[*] Norman Wirzba, "Noah and the Ark: Becoming Creation," *Living Pulpit* 9, no. 2 (April–June 2000): 28.
[†] The fifth sense of taste does not really fit into the aspect of visible prayer, even though the taste of a fresh peach is considered by some to be divine!

Sounds can be organic or created. Simply put, the sounds of nature such as birds, wind, and crickets are organic. Water is also considered organic and can be manipulated to vary its intensity and type of sound. We can create sounds in our garden with wind chimes or have intrusive created sounds from cars, machinery, or joyously boisterous teens.

When introducing a sound into your space, ask yourself how the sound affects you mentally and spiritually. One client intentionally tosses hard-shelled nuts to the squirrels in her yard. She delights in watching the squirrels scurry onto a branch and hearing them crunching away. Yet another friend is completely distracted and compulsively distressed by any sounds of chewing.

Nature produces a cacophony of sounds, some of which you can manipulate. I enjoy the sounds of birds singing and chirping when I am in a garden. I do not enjoy the shrill whistle from a cardinal or the screech of an irritated blue jay right over my head. To direct avian friends elsewhere, place the birdbath, houses, or feeders (with the exception of those for hummingbirds) at a distance from where you'll sit.

Sounds from water vary in type and intensity. With moving water, the faster the flow over rocks or the higher the fall from the edge of a fountain, the more noticeable the sound will be. If your spiritual elements include a fountain, you'll hear the flow and fall of water. A pool or pond of still water may have the soft sound of a bird bathing or a frog plopping into it.

From your table in chapter 2, if you listed it, what did you identify that you liked about water? Was it trickling and soft or flowing and distinct? Did you find that a still pool was more suited to your needs or a gurgling fountain more to your liking?

For some individuals the sound of water is distracting. An attendee at one of my programs shared with others in the group her sense that running water meant washing dishes, and she always felt compelled to get up and do her housework. For another participant, a garden design that included a fountain and pond had to be changed because of a trauma memory. Obviously, neither of these folks found spirituality when they sat next to flowing water.

There are other sounds to consider that could affect your contemplative area. Some cannot be avoided as, in my situation, the noise of cars and trucks on a busy road. For a friend who lives near a large metropolis, it is the sounds of jets from the airport a short distance away. Do you live next to a playground or school with alarm bells? Is there a railroad crossing a block away?

If you do have sounds that you want to minimize, try locating your garden space as far from the source as possible and install a succession of sound-absorbing plantings to reduce some of the noise. Tall and thick arborvitae (*Thuja* spp.) work very well where deer are not an issue; as do tall ornamental grasses, or any tall dense shrub.

Deaden the sound bouncing off a building by buffering its reflective wall surface. Inside a house you would use drapes and carpeting to deaden the sound. In your garden, you could use a line of sound-absorbing plants as mentioned above, trellised plants, or hanging wicker mats.

SIGHT, VISUAL INTERESTS, AND COLOR

Visually pleasing landscape design incorporates several elements, such as mass, form, repetition, line, and texture. If you have property that is intentionally landscaped, you will want to be sensitive to how your prayer space fits into the whole of your yard.

The anchor or focal point was mentioned earlier, and you noted what your desired element of visual interest would be. As a reminder, you could have selected a water feature, sacramental object, rocks, or maybe the view of your home as the focal point for prayer.

In this book, we will take a myopic view of your space. For a more thorough understanding of these and additional concepts of design, search the internet for reputable blog sites or reference books.

Color is very influential in a prayer space. The spiritual associations of color are personal, expansive, and cultural. Colors can evoke memories and associations.

A favorite green in the garden, and one that I use often, is the soft blue-green leaves of sage (*Salvia officinalis*) and lavender (*Lavandula* spp.). I spent a lot of time with my maternal grandmother, and this was the color on most of the walls in her house. As an adolescent in Detroit when the race riots erupted, the calming effect of being in her home during those turbulent times is a memory that reminds me to be still and trust in the general goodness of others.

With pencil in hand as you go through an overview of color, make note on the journal pages at the end of this chapter about what memories or feelings come to the surface. "Truly seeing color in the spiritual garden reminds us that our range of perception is broader than our range of expression."* You may not have the exact words to express why a color is more personal for you. What matters is that the feelings evoked by a color meet the desired response for your prayer space.

COLOR WHEEL

The color wheel is a circular diagram in which primary and usually intermediate colors are arranged sequentially so that related colors are next to each other and complementary colors are opposite. Even though this is more of a design issue, it's important to address how groupings of colors affect the emotions in the space you are planning.

Here is a basic reminder of some terminology.

In the color wheel, the first three colors are the primary ones from which all other colors are created. There are three: yellow, red, and blue. Primary colors evoke more intense feelings.

Then there are three secondary colors: orange, purple, and green. These colors tend to blend the emotions of the primary colors. An example is where yellow, which is intense and brings excitement, is combined with blue, which is reflective and detached, to create green, which tends to discourage intensity of focus and brings you to a sense of restfulness.

Six tertiary colors result from the combination of primary and secondary colors, such as blue-green, red-orange, and so on. These complete the twelve-part color wheel. Like secondary colors, tertiary colors too are a blending of feelings that the combined colors convey.

Harmonious or analogous colors are any two to four colors that are side-by-side on a twelve-part color wheel, such as yellow-green, yellow, and yellow-orange. One of the three colors is usually predominating visually, such as the clear orange of Pot Marigold *Calendual officinalis*, and is accented by other harmonious colors such as red-orange daylily *Hem-*

---

* Peg Streep, *Spiritual Gardening: Creating Sacred Space Outdoors* (Time Life Education, 2003), 27.

erocallis 'Christmas Is' and yellow-orange Signet Marigold *Tagetes signata* 'Pumila'. Harmonious color combinations, as the name implies, often convey a sense of peace — of being in harmony.

Complementary colors are any two colors directly opposite each other on a color wheel, such as red and green or red-purple and yellow-green. These opposing colors create maximum contrast and stability or balance. They create a sense of excitement, give drama, and add tension.

Take a moment and recall the purpose of your sacred space. Did you want to create a sense of excitement and revitalizing energy (complementary colors) or a sense of release to find calm (harmonious colors)?

Monochromatic refers to a single color hue in a range of tints (mov-

AdobeStock image

ing toward pastels) and shades (moving toward darker tones). A garden with all blues flowers would be considered monochromatic. Similar to a harmonious garden, it not only uses the colors next to each other on the color wheel, but also includes lighter and darker hues.

The emotional energy of the garden will depend on the color choice. If you want to feel invigorated in your garden, use warm colors such as red-oranges, orange, peach, and tangy yellow. If you want to feel calm, then go for cooler colors like blues, grays, and silver.

It is hard to create a monochromatic garden but when done well the results can be elegant. Be careful though: Monochromatic gardens can often be seen as indulgent, fall into the realm of garish when using bright colors, or appear muddied if using darker ones.

Polychromatic includes a riot of colors that creates a festive and party-like feel to a garden, especially when used with high-value colors. This color scheme is often used in children's gardens and memorials.

Cool colors are at the green-blue-violet end of the spectrum and are more soothing and calming than red-orange-yellows. Cool colors appear to blend and seem to disappear when seen at a distance, and so should be used for viewing up close.

Warm colors are at the red-orange-yellows end of the spectrum and are more invigorating and exciting than cool colors. These colors stand out when viewed from a distance, and the yellows and oranges appear to draw light into shade gardens.

Pastels are lighter tones (tints of white) and impart a softening and calming of the main color. Pastels, like most warm colors, will help draw light into deeply shaded areas.

More saturated colors are considered bold or vibrant, and are tied to stronger emotions, and unsaturated ones are softer and less striking. Strong sunlight can visually wash out softer colors. Highly saturated and intense colors, including richer greens, work best in full sun gardens viewed during midday.

Green is the most abundant color in the garden. Green symbolizes the virtue of hope and represents growth, fertility, renewal, harmony, tranquility, restfulness, and balance. It is an alluring and enticing color in that it can make us pause and mentally breathe even before we are conscious we need to do so.

Blue leads us to the infinite world beyond. Blue is contemplative and cooling. It represents sky and water. It directs our perspective outwards — a looking beyond. Blue is used to calm and relax and encourages openness, communication, and prayer.

Purple is a meditative color, a color of purpose. It combines the calmness, coolness, and expansiveness of blue with the focus and energy of red. It is a creative color we associate with inspiration and triumph.

Red is the warmest of all colors and symbolizes energy, intensity, and fiery passion. It is extroverted activity, vitality, strength, and prosperity. Dark burgundy reds represent mystery. It is the opposite of blue in the emotive spectrum. Because of the amount of energy in the color red, use it sparingly in a contemplative garden.

Orange has the primary characteristic of enhancing curiosity and exploration. It is indicative of change, a dynamic of thoughtful change rather than the explosive nature of red, and it suggests increased creativity and energy.

Yellow is pure, bright, and the easiest of all colors to see. It is full of intellectual energy, symbolizing wisdom, joy, happiness, attentiveness, and illumination. It brings awareness and clarity to the mind.

White is the color of the Holy Spirit, of truth and sanctity. It represents purity, innocence, and kindness. I read somewhere that white teaches us about relationships because, in our perceptions of colors, it tints how we see. White is in itself not a color but the complete revealed energy (manifestation) of all the colors — a very nice explanation of the completeness of the Holy Spirit. Use 10 percent white in your garden to make other colors stand out.

Black is perceived as mysterious, suggesting possibility. In psychology, black is the void that is full of hidden potential. Like white, it is in itself not a color; black is the absorption of all colors. It conceals them. Deep saturated raisin-purple is considered the black in a garden. It does not work well in shaded areas. Use black sparingly, as an accent, and plant this color up close for viewing.

Gray is the color of emptiness, a lack of movement and emotion. It also conveys restfulness, maturity, and security. It will stabilize more vibrant colors. Gray- or silver-leaved plants give the eye a place to rest in the garden.

FRAGRANCE

Our sense of smell can focus our attention immediately. Fragrance can be overt and intoxicating as in the scent of Stargazer lilies (*Lilium* 'Stargazer') or as subtle as the smell of freshly turned soil. Scents can create emotions that are on the surface of our psyches or elicit memories that we have repressed. Scent is universal, but what a person considers as fragrant is very personal.

How will you plan to incorporate this sense in your prayer space? In your chart from chapter 2 you identified fragrances you liked and how they are dispersed. Look now at how you would like to use them.

Fragrances come to us from all levels in the garden: underfoot, near our bodies when we brush them with our legs or hands, or surrounding us in the air from aromatic plantings. Fragrances are also seasonal: crushed leaves when walking in the autumn, lilacs in late spring, or an herb garden on a hot summer afternoon.

If you like incense or other burnt offerings be sure to identify them in your notes. A trail of smoke from incense or a small fire offers a visual stimulus as well. In many cultures the trail of smoke is associated with rising prayers and transitions.

TOUCH

The textures of plants may be part of what leads you to prayer. A pot of woolly Lamb's Ear (*Stachys byzantina* 'Silky Fleece') next to your bench could help alleviate tension when you stroke its thick fuzzy leaves. Maybe the feathery touch of dill and its resulting aroma as your hand brushes against it will stimulate memories of making pickles with your grandmother. What would the touch of the soft bark of a beech tree (*Fagus* spp.) bring to mind?

I remember being delightfully surprised one late fall day by my emotions when touching the smooth silvery-green bark of a mature curly willow (*Salix matsudana* 'Tortuosa'). It was soft and had been warmed from the sun and had thousands of distinct petioles forming little yellow-green diamonds all along its stems. As I stood there in awe, letting the tears wash over me, a familiar story about St. Francis of Assisi came to mind. While he was walking down a farm lane one early winter day, Francis was deeply frustrated about his inability to reach the souls of many townspeople. As he approached a leafless apple tree he raised his arm, grabbed a barren limb and shouted at it, "Teach me of God!" and as the miracle is recorded, the tree immediately burst into bloom.

We are touched by touching God. How will you bring this sense to life? Is touch part of what draws you to prayer?

Your notes from this chapter have helped you understand how your senses will affect designing your prayer space. The next chapter will help you incorporate what you have identified with other visual influences of design.

JOURNAL

What colors work well with the focus of your garden as identified in chapter 2? Which of your five senses deepens your awareness of God? Is it one in particular or the combination of your senses that does so?

What memories of scents or colors do you find calming? invigorating?

How will the emotional energy of color, scent, or sound affect you spiritually in the garden?

8
Basic Building Blocks of Design

I think this is what hooks one to gardening: it is the closest one can come to being present at creation.

— Phyllis Theroux

In landscape architecture there are specific design elements used to create beautiful and amazing outdoor spaces. Formal training and numerous books are dedicated to this art.

Note the first word of this chapter's heading — *basic*. This is the approach that we will take in fostering the design of your small garden space. One of the best workbooks I have found and often recommend to the beginner for planning a home landscaping — though it is an older publication — is *Designing Your Gardens and Landscapes: 12 Simple Steps for Successful Planning* by Janet Macunovich (Storey, 2000).

In this chapter I will give simple explanations and examples for each of the design elements. Included at the end of this section is a worksheet

I use in gardening programs. Recreate it or fill it in as you read this chapter to help you refine the plans for your own prayer space. You may, like some of the participants in my classes, be surprised by the spiritual influence certain elements carry. Once you have filled in the spaces of your form with your notes, add it to your binder.

MASS, FORM, AND SHAPE

These elements are very interrelated. *Mass* is the amount of area and *form* or *shape* is the geometric configuration that the mass portrays. Let's take for example two kinds of spruce trees: A Cranston Spruce (*Picea abies* 'Cranstonii') can grow to 50'/15 m high and 30'/9 m wide whereas a Dwarf Alberta Spruce (*Picea glauca* 'Conica') usually only grows to 8'/2.4 m high and about 3–4'/1–1.25 m wide. Now both of these spruce trees have the same distinct form, being a triangular shape, yet the mass of the Cranston is significantly greater than the mass of the Dwarf Alberta Spruce.

An additional consideration of form and shape is with flowers. This applies to how the flowers are held on the stem and their overall appearance. Consider the mounded form of both the Annabelle Hydrangea (*Hydrangea arborescens* 'Annabelle') shrub and clump forming perennial Fireworks Goldenrod (*Solidago rugosa* 'Fireworks'). With the hydrangea the form of the flower is a ball or globe shape, and the goldenrod flowers form is a lance or linear shape. Also note that the round mass of the hydrangea bloom is greater than the mass of the linear goldenrod bloom.

LINE

This directs the mind, the eye, and the direction you will move. It includes how a path is laid out, how your eye follows the layering of plants, and how calm or stimulating a space may feel. Spaces with curved lines have a softer shape and are more calming than those that have straight lines and angles, being more stimulating. The way your garden beds are laid out includes both the line and shape.

A focal point is defined as where your eye will go first and rest for a moment. Often the line of a garden will create a focal point or lead you to one. You will recall in chapter 2 that you had initially established what would be the focal point in your prayer garden.

TEXTURE AND CONTRAST

Texture is relative and comparative to another surface. Ornamental grasses are considered finer in texture when compared to broader leaf plants like oak trees (*Quercus* spp.) or hostas but are considered coarser in texture when contrasted with the herb dill (*Anethum graveolens*).

Contrast is similar to texture in that it is the association of two dissimilar objects and can also refer to form, line, or color (i.e., round or linear, coarse or fine, curved or straight, saturated or pastel).

A note about texture: The viewing gradient of texture (i.e., the layering of plants in a vertical interest) from fine to coarse will visually reduce an area and make things appear closer, and often increases the sense of privacy or intimacy.

To expand the visual appearance of a small area, do the opposite and move from course to medium to fine textures. To do this, mentally break up a small space into thirds. Place the shorter, most coarsely textured materials closest to you in the first third of the area. In the remaining area, place the medium-textured plants in the middle and then the tallest finer-textured plants behind them, the farthest from where you will view them. You will want to use a bit more finely textured plants than medium-textured ones in this back part of your garden.

COLOR

Color is a supporting element to the other building blocks. This feature of design can be understood by looking at a black and white photo of a well-designed garden. The forms, lines, and textures present a sense of balance and unity. Remember to take black and white pictures while creating your own garden.

If you look at the same picture in color, its deeper beauty is revealed by the way color enhances the boldness of an element. Remember from the previous chapter that color elicits emotions. If we take, for example, the line and texture of a large-leaved hosta, the feel of a garden will change with the color of its leaf — silver-blue, kelly green, or bright chartreuse — even with hosta that are of similar size and shape.

REPETITION

Repetition is the reoccurrence of an element throughout the garden. It can be the color of a flower that is also seen on a chair or globe, or several of the same plant throughout the garden. Even the bricks used on a building can be repeated in edging or paths and will help unify the space. Everything seems to be more cohesive when the thread of repetition is woven into a garden.

COMPOSITION

Composition is the principle of bringing the preceding elements into harmony by using scale, balance, rhythm, emphasis, and simplicity.

Scale is relative to size, using the average height of a person as the reference point. Something is out of scale when the transition of elements is too abrupt and the object appears too small or too big in its surroundings. A negative example of scale would be an arbor that has a fourteen-foot-high arch and only a four-foot width. Its height looks very disproportionate to its width — like a shoebox on end — even when placed near tall trees.

Balance has to do with visual weight and incorporates some of the concepts of scale. We understand what it means to balance physical weights on a bar with a fulcrum underneath; balance can be obtained with multiple smaller objects at one end counterbalancing one larger object. This is the same principle only visually. An example here would be balancing out a tall tree with a wide flower bed nearby.

Nature is asymmetrical and informal, so creating balance has a lot to do with composing and arranging objects in a similar way. It is delightful to watch how people will intuitively seek to create balance in a garden and not know why one arrangement is more pleasing than another. The balance comes from the visual weight of objects seeming to be equal.

Rhythm is similar to repetition in that it adds a sense of unity and cohesiveness to a space. It is the predictability in the repeating of elements. Imagine the rhythm in a long straight path where every eight feet there grows a bright yellow clump of Hakone grass (*Hakonechloa macra* 'Aureola').

Emphasis is also known as the focal point in landscape architecture.

You can also consider the intent of your sacred garden as the emphasis or focus of your larger garden.

Simplicity is achieved by limiting the variety and kinds of elements, such as plants and materials, used in the design of your prayer space. Remember how you have been refining your ideas in each chapter? You have been simplifying your design.

This is a lot of information to process, so take small bites and use the work sheet to help you along. Much of what you will use in designing your small retreat space will feel intuitive. The difference is that now you have the words that coincide with what you already knew.

DESIGN ELEMENTS WORKSHEET

Element/Form	Emotional Connection	Your Notes
Shape		
Triangle	Sharp, tense, strong	
Square	Rigid, stable, fixed	
Rectangle	Stable, directed, purposeful	
Circle	Quiet, softness, unbroken, perfect	
Free Form	Casual, imperfect, loose	
Line		
Straight	Formal, firm, stationary	
Angled, squared	Stress, tension, excitement	
Curved	Relaxed, gentleness, flowing	
Texture		
Coarse	Informal, bold, will maintain quality at a distance and appear closer	

Fine (Small garden, ⅔ fine to ⅓ coarse)	Restraint, quietness, refinement; will lose its quality at a distance and appear smoother	
Plant Shape		
Spiked/Vertical	Energy, persistence	
Round/Mound	Serene, cheerful	
Horizontal/Prostrate	Grounded, openness	
Conical/Pyramidal	Firmness, stability, secure	
Vase/Flaring	Transition, excitement	
Climbing	Movement, reaching, expansiveness	
Weeping	Quietness, calming, softness	
Irregular	Playful, open	

JOURNAL

What design elements evoke a spiritual connection in your heart?

Which design elements and layouts for your garden will enhance your focus in prayer?

9
Hardscape

How fair is the garden amid the trials and passions of existence.

— Benjamin Disraeli

The hardscape is the non-plant materials in your garden. It includes such things as rocks, walkways, seating, containers, trellises or obelisks, sacramental objects or art, and buildings or structures. You have already identified what hardscape features and other elements you want in your garden and have been clipping pictures of each of them, creating a wish list of sorts. Here is how to narrow down your choices and get a better understanding of your personal style.

Remember those pockets you filled with collected pictures and clippings? Go back to them, one at a time, and look at each collection by topic. Lay all the clippings for that topic on a table and look them over, because now it's time to narrow them down. This is easy if you're the rare person who only has a half-dozen or so to sort through.

Looking at what you have laid out, try to find the theme in all of them. Some of the images will not seem to match what you had defined in chapter 2. Decide if your analysis from the chart you created earlier is weak or if your images are impulse snips — nice-to-haves that do not necessarily fit in with your spiritual needs. Ultimately, you will want to narrow down the number of images to only a few for each theme.

Take your time to think about what it is you have defined as an essential element. Of all the images in front of you, discard your least favorite one. Of those that are remaining, discard again until you have only three or four left. A very clear picture of what you like for your prayer space will emerge from this process.

Take those remaining pictures and tape or glue them to a piece of paper, add any comments or notes, and add this sheet to your notebook. Continue to do so for each pocket of your essential elements.

You will want to consider your budget. Of the elements you have selected, which ones are highest in priority for you? Rate them at the top of the pages on which you have glued the illustrations.

Which of these elements can you acquire now, even though they may be third or fourth on your list of essentials? Consider a short-term solution for an expensive item until it can be purchased. Can you get by with a green plastic chair and table for a few summers until you can afford the curved willow cane seats and side table? Maybe you like the looks of a wrought-iron obelisk. Can you paint a wooden one black or cobalt blue for the time being?

If you are creating a public prayer space, you are probably working within a strict budget. Your desires may include a fountain or sculpture, granite benches, and a nice paved walkway. If the fountain or sculpture you've selected works best but is more expensive than what was allocated for it, consider adjusting down other items. Can slat benches be used while you fundraise for the granite ones? Can a gravel walkway suffice until pavers can be bought?

Gardens grow — and not only the plants in them. Immediate gratification is a rare event with gardens or the soul. So, take the time to decide for yourself what is most necessary for your contemplative space.

Your garden of visible prayer is coming to life!

JOURNAL

What are the foundational beliefs in your life that lend structure to your faith?

10
Plant Selection

You created all things, and now you provide for their growth.
May we always perceive your handiwork in creation.

— The *Liturgy of the Hours*, Tuesday in the 19th
Week in Ordinary Time, Intercessions

Plant selection is one of the more rewarding occupations of garden design. Getting just that right plant in the right place — visually, physiologically, and spiritually — is fulfilling. In a garden space that is small, it is a matter of preference whether to select plants before you have your garden's design drawn out or after. Keep track of the plants you intsall with the information sheets at the back of the book

As you progress through this book, the Christian symbolism associated with plants will be important, especially for a spiritually themed garden. In *A Garden Catechism* you will find one hundred plants with the broadest range of application in a garden that are familiar representations in Christian art, architecture, metaphors, and parables, or expressed in folklore.

That book includes a variety of moral and religious themes, sentimentalities, and legends associated with a plant. Catechetical information includes how a particular plant connects to our Faith, the story behind its moniker, and its use in conveying the story of our Church. There is a vast array of symbolic plants, many culturally based in Christian history. A plant may have various though similar and sometimes conflicting meanings, but don't let the ascribed symbolism limit your use of the plant.

Similarly to how a single word in one's *lectio divina* may hit you like lightning to the soul, a plant may speak to you in a spiritually unique way — so use it! Focus on *why* you are drawn to it, why it brings you delight and brings a God-spark to your spirituality. If that plant draws you closer to God in the garden then it can only enrich your prayer life.

When selecting plants before drawing out your design, you will start by creating a plant vocabulary for the site. This is a list of the plants that you like and will grow in that location, and whose symbolism fits into the theme of your prayer garden. Not all of the plants listed will be used, but you will have a set of options when you need them.

If you draw your design first, laying in paths, seating, and other hardscape elements, you will know that you want a shrub here or ornamental grasses there. After you have done this simple drawing you will go to your garden books, including *A Garden Catechism*, and select specific plants. The next chapter will guide you in creating your drawings.

Whatever is easiest for you to do — selecting the plants first or drawing the space — do it. Whatever allows your creative nature to flow, follow it. I have used either method for creating prayer gardens and have found them both to be successful.

If your sacred space will use container plantings instead of an installed garden your task will be much simpler. Only a portion of what follows will apply. Not only do you have a smaller plant vocabulary to create, you also have the added benefit of changing the plantings from season to season.

For an installed garden you will need to know what Hardiness Zone you live in. This will tell you what plants will survive in your area (zone). There are both cold and heat considerations for hardiness. A Hardiness Zone tells you that a plant grown in that area can endure a 50 percent kill-off of its root because of temperature and still survive; keep in mind that if that happens repeatedly the plant will die out. You might also check gardening resources in your area, such as your county extension office, garden clubs, or a reputable nursery to get accurate information.

PLANT VOCABULARY

You will now use the features in the site assessment you made in chapter 6. What had you concluded about shade and sunlight, and what areas are involved? What are the characteristics of the soil? Is the site dry because it is on a slope or in full sunlight? Will new plants have to contend with other stronger or established root systems?

To create a chart of your plant vocabulary, make a table with the plant's name on the side, then columns with the features of the site (which will be matched to a plant's horticultural needs) across the top of each column. The first column will be for the name of the plant. Each column should be labeled with the feature of the site: full sun, dense shade, dry, rocky, and the like. Be sure to include a column for plant symbolism, and garden theme if applicable.

Plant name: Lamb's Ear							
	Horticultural needs:	Full sun	Well drained	Sandy loam	NOTES: roots spread by rhizomes, needs room to expand	Plant symbolism: Meekness/ obedience, humility
	Garden site assessment (from ch. 6)	Afternoon shade	Slope	Sandy/ rocky	NOTES: Existing shrubs securing hillside	Garden theme: Stations of the Cross

Start your plant vocabulary by listing *existing* plants at your proposed prayer garden site. Not only will this help you familiarize yourself with using the table you have just created but it will assist you in looking up plants and becoming familiar with why they grow where they do. You will want to note if those existing plants are thriving or, if barely surviving, if they need to be relocated.

As you select a new plant, write its horticultural needs, the color and season of bloom if it flowers, and put a check mark in the column that matches its culture needs.

You may want to include columns that designate the texture of a plant, as well as its mature size (height and width) and form. Reference materials and labels that come with the plant will tell you the plant's mature size. The Design Elements Worksheet created in chapter 8 helps you to think about what forms, line, textures, and shapes work best for your spiritual space.

One of my key phrases, reiterated often in my gardening programs, is to select the right plant for the right place. You may love the yellow variegated color and texture of Hakone Grass (*Hakonechloa macra* 'Aureola') but it will be of no use planted in the western sun of a sandy site; it needs high shade and moist, well-drained soil.

I often found myself collecting pictures of plants as I collected ideas for a garden. If you too have collected pictures of flowers and shrubs, write the names of those plants in your table and record their characteristics.

A side note here: Many people will also include the symbolism of plants in their initial selection process. This feature is similar to the influential energy of colors. For example, to some people the birch tree (*Betula papyrifera*) is thought to signify rebirth and new beginnings; the carnation (*Dianthus* spp.), whose name literally means Flower of God, represents Mary and the Incarnation of Jesus.

Keep in mind that the meanings of a plant are culturally diverse and have different meanings in different religions: A person of Irish decent may have a very different association for poppies than someone from the Middle East. Definitely do research into the meanings or historical allusions associated with certain plants, especially in culturally specific public gardens. There are many resources available to help in the search, including *A Garden Catechism*.

As you progress through your design and selection process, keep it simple. I often teach new gardeners the rule of three:

- Three heights
- Three textures
- Three colors
- Three seasons

This simple rule applies both to containers and installed gardens, and will help you avoid being overwhelmed by the sheer number of available plant options. And everything does not need to flower. Not until recently were flowers considered the mainstay of a garden. Before that it was the form and texture of plants that defined a beautiful garden — flowers being the bonus and not the focus.

PLANTING OPTIONS

You have established the intent of your garden and what its style will be. Consider some of the following in your plant selection process.

Native Plants

When an area is located in a naturalistic setting, one option is to enhance your new garden by using native plants. For those of you who are ecologically minded — maybe dedicating your garden to Saint Fiacre or Saint Francis — this will enhance your connectedness to the system of nature already in place. The other benefit of working with native plants is that they will require less support from you because they are already matched to the environment having a reduced need for fertilization, disease control, and watering. Native plants will also encourage local birds and butterflies into your prayer space.

Reduced Pollen

If you have allergies or an aversion to bees, look for information on allergy-free gardening. In creating a garden for the visually impaired, use this information to draw bees and other pollinators away from areas where people may be in danger of being stung if they touch certain plants.

Night or Moon Gardens

It is a challenge, but a very fulfilling one, to design a garden like this, especially if you will be using your space after sunset. Look for flowers that are very light pastels, or better yet all-white, that bloom in the evening (check local resources for your zone), and mix in leaves that are very light and/or variegated. It can take your breath away to see a garden glowing in the moonlight.

Potager

The kitchen garden is a popular concept that has come in to its own in the United States but has existed in Europe for centuries. In monasteries the potager was an integral part of monastic life and included medicinal and culinary herbs, food for the table, and flowers for the altar. Sometimes thought of as an edible landscape, this kind of garden uses essential design elements when incorporating fruits and vegetables into the landscape. There are many associations with spirituality in a potager: the idea of being nourished, a reliance on the Creator and his bounty, a focus on family, and bearing fruit, to mention just a few.

Container Gardening

Planters offer a great deal of diversity. You can use containers exclusively on porches and decks or incorporate them into an existing garden space. You can use planters to resolve problems when soils are unworkable from compaction, contamination, or tree roots.

Container gardens are helpful in other ways, too. Once I had to design a garden in a section of soil that was next to a sidewalk leading to a main entrance. Heavy equipment had compacted the soil, and the soil had been contaminated with oils and cleaning solvents. This rather large area would not support any plants, and I had to find a solution to the eyesore. Digging out and replacing the soil was too costly — not to mention trying to work around existing utility lines and trees.

To solve this problem I picked up and recycled oblong livestock watering troughs, drilled them for better drainage, set them in place, filled them with a shallow layer of gravel, half-filled them with composted material (decomposed plant waste) and then added eight inches of potting mix. I then enclosed the troughs with a decorative wood fencing and planted a variety of annuals and grasses in them. It was from this practice by many gardeners several decades ago that the now-popular metal and framed raised garden beds evolved. The next chapter will expand on the technique of creating container gardens.

Don't stop looking for plant combinations once your garden is created. Continue expanding your plant vocabulary for diversifying the plants in your sacred space as the years go by. You may find you want to add something more after you have used your area for a while or that you want to add something new to another part of your property.

JOURNAL

As you consider plants with specific symbolisms, which ones spoke most fully to your spiritual needs? List them here with a one or two sentence prayer.

1.

2.

3.

4.

5.

6.

7.

8.

9.

10.

11
Container Gardens

We are sowing seeds and it is up to him to bring the increase.

— Servant of God Dorothy Day

Making a container garden is simpler than most people think. By following a few rules, you can create a wonderful addition to your prayer space. You can also make an edible container garden using the same instructions.*

The containers you will use are usually chosen because of aesthetics, but let's also consider their function. There are some things to keep in mind about the containers themselves. Remember to consider the weight of a container, especially if you need to move it for winter storage. Also consider the color of your container. When exposed to direct sunlight a black or dark-colored exterior will get hot and increase the soil temperature inside the container, damaging the roots of many plants that are not heat-tolerant. To help prevent overheating you can choose a container of

---

* Rose Mary Nichols McGee and Maggie Stuckey, *The Bountiful Container* (Workman, 2002), though dated, is a great resource!

a lighter color. You can also place something in front of the container to shade it during the hottest part of the day. Another option is to insulate the inside walls of the container before filling it, using Styrofoam sheets cut into vertical strips.

The following chart will help you decide what will work best for your purpose.

CONTAINER TYPES

Container Type	Moisture Retention	Weight	UV Resistant	Winter
Clay/Ceramics	Average	Moderately heavy, smaller pieces moveable	Yes	Not winterproof, prone to freeze expansion damage
Concrete	Average to high, adequate drainage a must	Heavy, stationary	Yes	Usually winterproof
Fiber Grow Bags	Dries quickly	Light, if heavily filled may split when moved	Varies widely, check supplier	Usually winterproof

Fiberglass	Very high	Light, smaller pieces moveable	Not usually, check supplier	Not winterproof, prone to freeze expansion damage
Metal	Very high	Light to moderately heavy, usually moveable	Yes	Winterproof
Moss	Very low, use a reservoir inside container	Moderate, moveable depends on size	Yes, but … it is an organic medium that will deteriorate	Winterproof
Plastic	Very high	Very light, even for large pots	Usually not, check supplier	Not winterproof, prone to freeze expansion damage
Terra Cotta	Average	A bit heavy, larger pieces are stationary	Yes	Not winterproof
Wood	Average	Moderately heavy, usually moveable	Somewhat UV resistant	Not winterproof unless treated

When filling your container use only potting mix, not soil. Soil will compact and inhibit root development. Do not use filler in the bottom of larger pots. Research has shown that plants whose roots have grown into the air spaces of filler are weaker and prone to disease. If you do have a large container that you cannot afford to fill with potting mix, use a smaller container that will fit inside. Place an upended pot in the bottom of your large pot for your smaller pot to rest on or use bricks — which will also stabilize a container in windy areas — stacked to the optimum height. A smaller container inside a larger one is also a good solution for preventing the soil from overheating if you use a container that is dark in color.

With excessively large containers, as was the case with the recycled watering troughs mentioned in the previous chapter, add potting mix on top to a depth of eight inches. This is the depth of the root system of most annual plants. Fill the remaining lower portion with composted material, which is lighter than soils. It is not recommended to use cardboard in the bottom as filler because it creates a water barrier as it compresses.

If you are going to place your container on a wood deck, or for that matter any hard surface, be sure to raise the container at least a half inch off the surface. This will ensure that the container gets proper drainage and also prevents damage or stains on the surface where it is located. You can use any number of items to support the container, from coordinated footings that match the pot to recycled bricks.

When you design your container think about how it will be viewed when you are in your space. Will you see it from all sides? Do you intend to place it against a wall or in a corner? Will you use a series of containers to divide a space?

A container that is seen from all sides should have a circular design with the focal point at the center. A container placed against a wall or in a corner will look best in a half-moon design with the focal point near the back. If you intend to add an item to your container, such as a globe or statue, place it slightly forward from the center and elevated — as the plants grow you do not want them to hide the main attraction. When you line up large containers in a row, such as a divider for your prayer space, consider which side will be facing the sun. The taller plants in the middle of your container will shade the plants on the opposite side. Unless you plan on rotating your containers weekly, use shade-tolerant plants on that side.

Keep the design of your container simple by using the rule of three, as mentioned in chapter 10. You will want three colors, three textures, and three heights — one of which should be trailing so it will spill over the edge of the container.

You should decide how many plants to buy based on the plants' overall size at maturity. Read the plant tags to know how big the plants will get, and then purchase about a third more. The reasoning here is that you will want to create a lush container and container-grown plants rarely achieve their full growth. So, if it would take three plants to fill a garden space of the same size, add one more for your container and buy four.

Try to create a planting plan using odd numbers: that is, one in the middle, three at the next ring, and one to five on the outer edge depending on the size of the plant and your container. Odd numbers of plants are more pleasing and create less tension visually.

By applying what you have learned throughout this book and using that knowledge to create your container, you will create a beautiful addition for your sacred space.

Container Gardens

JOURNAL _____

As I am planning to plant, and planting, what am I learning about God's action as Creator and my own stewardship of the bit of the world that lies before me?

As a garden serves me in my spirituality and my prayer life, how can I serve God and the others around me?

12
Drawing It All Out

[The garden] doesn't have to be elaborate; it just has to be soulful.

— Nancy Endres[*]

You have collected all the information on what leads you to an outdoor place of solace. You have the pictures of where your space will be located, your worksheets have been filled in, the illustrations of the hardscape items have been culled, and a list of plant materials has been created from which you have narrowed materials down to a select few. You can now start to pull everything together.

For those of you placing your retreat area on a deck or porch, your drawing efforts will be minimal. You will use the plan view described below for creating your containers.

Landscape architecture is designed with two drawing views: elevation view and plan view. The elevation drawing is oriented from eye level looking directly at the area to give you a sense of scale, line, and form/mass; that is, you draw the house with the shrub under the window and

---

[*] Nancy Endres, "The Healing Garden," *Midwest Living* (2005): 110.

the rock in front of the shrub. The plan drawing is looking down on the area as if from a bird's-eye or aerial view. These eventually become your planting plan.

CREATING A WORKSHEET

This section will help you create worksheets to be used for drawing your designs. How to draw each view, step-by-step, will come a little later in the chapter.

For creating the elevation view you should already have a picture looking directly at your chair and another picture, as if you were standing behind the chair. This is unlike the plan view, where you will consider all of the area at once.

If you can, have the individual photos of your area each enlarged to an 8½" x 11" image. Be sure to crop the pictures first to include a fairly narrow view of the space (you really don't need a lot of lawn or the whole driveway in the picture). Lay a piece of tracing paper over your enlarged picture, and trace a general outline of the area, your chair, and any significant features such as existing trees or arbors. Make several tracings or copies of the general outline for each picture. These will be your worksheets for the elevation view.

Drawing the plan view is usually done after the elevation view sketches have been selected. To create the worksheet for your plan view you will need to measure off the width and depth of the space and draw in existing elements and their sizes. It is important to be fairly accurate. Usually these drawings are done on small squares of graph paper. To make it easy to draw to scale, you could use a 1:1 scale where 1'/30 cm equals 1"/3 cm.

Yes, this is math, but as Scripture says, do not be afraid.

Expect to make several drawings of each view as you play with your ideas. All these drawings will help you decide what you like or don't like.

ELEVATION VIEW

Start drawing by placing your hardscape images in front of you on your work area, and then get the looking-from- and directly-in-front-of-chair view of your elevated worksheet tracings. When you draw, try to keep the scale of the objects in mind as best you can. Do not worry about drawing things perfectly. Remember that most of us are not artists and besides, nobody else needs to see your drawings.

Your tracing already has the chair in it, so draw the seating you want for your garden over it, and then add the larger foundation items such as the arbor, trees, water feature, or gates.

Once you have the foundation (also known as *background*) in place you can begin to layer the mid-sized items like bird baths, boulders, and so on and finish with the smaller hardscape details. Remember to draw in a path if you have one. Do the same with the other elevation view. You will find that you are drawing one thing on top of another: That is *exactly* the right thing to be doing. Try using colored pencils for each layer and erase background lines as you go.

Repeat this process with your plant material, using the size of a nearly mature plant as your guide. Set the pictures you have collected on your work area along with the plant list chart. Starting with the foundation plants, draw those that are taller at the back of the view, then draw in the mid-sized plants and lastly the smaller plants which will be in front. Use capital letters to identify which plants will go where; that is, daylilies are marked with an *A*, groundcover with a *B*, and so on. Write the corresponding letter next to the plant's name on the list.

Unless you're very good at drawing you should have a lot of messy-looking layouts. Look over each set of your elevation views. As before, pull your least favorite layout from the lineup and discard it. Continue this process, redrawing if necessary, until you are satisfied with one layout for each elevation view.

PLAN VIEW

The plan view drawings take less time. You already have the correct dimensions, existing structures, and plants drawn. You will transfer the images from the elevation view drawings to your plan view. Working with the elevation views you decided to keep, draw the seating, path, water feature, and other hardscape elements on to your plan view.

As before, try to keep your elements to scale. There are special rulers and templates available if you know how to calculate and use them. If not, try this procedure:

1. Let's say your retreat area is 8' x 6' (3 m x 2 m): Convert that to 8" x 6" (30 cm x 20 cm) on your paper. (This is a 1:1 scale.)
2. Draw in any existing structures using the 1:1 scale.
3. You may know the size of your chair or bench or table; draw that in at the 1:1 scale.
4. Do this again for your walkway or arbor.

That's all there is to it! You now have an idea of how the measurements of 1:1 will scale down items as you draw them in your plan. Keep this in mind as you add in plants.

With many plants, especially annuals and perennials, overlapping them a little or planting them in a group will create a different appearance (mass and form) as the plants mature. You see this in many gardens where there are multiples of the same plant put together to create a mound of color. If the selected plant is tall, to stand alone in a collection, it is enhanced by allowing a slight space between them.

Again, make as many drawings as you can. Follow the same procedure as before: Pull out and discard your least favorite layouts until you have your final plan view.

You will use this final drawing to make your shopping list for materials and plants. It is also your planting plan as you begin installation.

JOURNAL

Write a metaphor about how culling things in your life enhances your faith journey.

UNIT 3
DEVELOP

13
Preparation and Installation

*Who bends the knee where violets grow
A hundred Secret Things shall know.*

— Rachel Field[*]

The anticipation of getting to this point has accompanied you through each step in your discernment and design process of your outdoor prayer space. Finally — and with a full appreciation of this process and a careful assembling of your notes — the emergence of your sacred space is about to take place!

Preparation of the site for creating a new garden space is more intensive than adapting an existing garden or adding to part of a structure. In preparing your site, try to think about the fact that you are in a sense creating holy ground. Offer up your efforts to acknowledge spiritual movement and to foster a sense of sanctuary. This is not just another pretty space.

Later in the process you can include children, family, or friends in

---
[*] Rachel Field, *Hitty: Her First Hundred Years* (Macmillan, 1929).

creating your retreat area if you need assistance or want them to share in the installation process. But at first, begin this process quietly, alone with the Holy Spirit.

The last item to be brought into your space is the object that you had previously selected as the meditative or prayer focus. When you introduce this item into your garden, such as an incense burner, statue, or specific plant, it will complete the development process.

NON-GARDEN ADAPTATION

With an area that is part of an existing porch or deck, there are a few things you can do to help you mentally envision the area as a sanctuary. Begin by taking all movable objects from the space, even those items that you will be using. Then sweep. Yes, I know it seems obvious that you'll want to get rid of the dirt, but there is more to this than removing debris. Imagine that you are spiritually sweeping away the abrasiveness and hardness, the darkness and struggles, the disruption and chaos of daily living.

Having swept out the debris, cleanse the area. Not necessarily with bucket and mop (though maybe the porch could use a good wash!) but with a sacramental purification:

> Sacramentals do not confer the grace of the Holy Spirit in the way that the sacraments do, but by the Church's prayer, they prepare us to receive grace and dispose us to cooperate with it. "For well-disposed members of the faithful, the liturgy of the sacraments and sacramentals sanctifies almost every event of their lives with the divine grace which flows from the Paschal mystery of the Passion, Death, and Resurrection of Christ. From this source all sacraments and sacramentals draw their power. There is scarcely any proper use of material things which cannot be thus directed toward the sanctification of men and the praise of God." (*Catechism of the Catholic Church,* 1670)

This purification of your space can be as simple as sprinkling holy water or blessed salt, or burning blessed incense; or it can be as elaborate as having a priest come to bless it. Pray and converse with the Lord as you do this. Don't skip this step, even though it may initially feel awkward.

When you have completed this cleansing, the first item to bring into your area will be the seating, or if this is your selected prayer item, bring an alternate chair or bench. Following your drawings, place your hardscape items where they belong. Use your seating as a reference point so you can check the view to be certain you like the results.

Now, if you had designed for them, install your plants along the edge of your area or put your container of plants in place. You may find, as all designers do, that slight adjustments may be needed once you sit and look around at your work.

Once you are satisfied with your efforts, quietly and with prayerfulness bring the object that represents your meditative focus into your area.

IN-GROUND GARDEN INSTALLATION

The process you use is the same as for any landscape installation, with the added Christian dimension of being accompanied by the Holy Spirit as you do so.

Begin to mentally sanctify the area by removing debris, pulling weeds, turning the soil, or by doing some other sort of personal preparatory activity. As you work imagine that you are removing from your area those disruptions that press down on your peace and centeredness.

After you have prayed your way through preparing the area spiritually, ask others to assist as needed.

With your drawing in hand, place the seating where you intend it to be or use something similar on which to sit as you work. Mark off your garden outline, paths, and/or beds. One of my favorite ways to do this is the familiar garden hose trick: Lay the hose on the ground in the outline you desire and mark the outline using spray paint, bone meal, or any organic material that will visually designate a line when the hose is lifted.

If you are creating a new or unusually shaped flower bed, narrowly trench out your outline using a spade and remove unwanted plants or sod. Any soil amendments should be added at this time; compost is always a good thing.

The next phase is more labor intensive. At this point you install your hardscape and any large ornamental trees. This will include everything from walkways and edgings to permanent structures. When laying pavers or using cement for posts, check references for proper installation. If you intend to lay a ground cloth as a weed barrier, do so after these main features are in place.

As you work out the bones of your space, be sure to sit back at times and observe your progress. Do this from the location of your preferred garden seat. This will allow you to look at your drawings and check the view to ensure that all is going according to your plan. As I already mentioned, all designs are tweaked along the way, so remain confident in the drawings you have developed knowing that minor site-related adjustments will occur.

Before you begin the last phase in installation, take a few minutes to look around your small space from inside the retreat area. Are you feeling content with what you have done? Have you relocated the garbage cans or dug out that shrub you really didn't want? Are all but your designated objects in place as you planned? Is the water feature or gate or lighting working properly? Take the time to breathe; this is your place of solace. It is an interior view of your personal sacred journey on many levels.

As you prepare for planting remember that you will work from the center toward the outside, from tallest to the shortest, from the farthest to the nearest.

On the afternoon before you intend to put plants in or transplant them, thoroughly water them. This will help reduce the stress of transplanting. For more information about transplanting, see the section "From Pot to Garden" in chapter 15. If it hasn't rained in a several days and your soil seems dry when you dig about four inches down below the surface, in the area you will be planting add 1 in/2.5 cm of water about twenty-four hours beforehand. Evenly moist but not wet soil is easier to work and, again, reduces the stress to plants. If you think that the afternoon sun will be too intense for your new plants, put them in later in the day — there is no rule saying that you have to garden in the mornings — or construct a sun barrier with a white sheet and bamboo poles.

When the area is properly moist it is time to get planting. Leaving your plants in their pots, place them in your garden area as indicated by your plan drawing. You will often find it necessary to adjust the potted plants after you get them set in place — maybe one is too close to the fence or another grouping is too tight; keep in mind the mature size of your plant as you work. Be sure to rotate the plants so the nicest side faces the viewer, or that the shape of the branches forms a pleasing visual line that you can see from where you will be sitting.

If you are working through ground cloth, or other forms of ground covering, cut an X about 25 percent larger than the hole you will dig where you intend to plant. Tuck the flaps under the remaining material, dig, plant, and water.

To prevent damage to the smaller plants designated in your plan, wait until after the larger ones are in the ground to place them.

Oftentimes smaller plants are purchased in trays or flats of trays. Individual plants in these types of carriers are sometimes called *plugs*. Don't pop them out of their trays just yet. Set the entire pack in the area where those plugs will be planted. Once you are satisfied with their arrangement, put them in the ground too, spaced according to their mature size.

If you intend to use mulch* you should work from one side to the other from back to front. Here is a trick to help with spreading it. Remember all those pots from the plants you just put in? After knocking out the excess dirt from inside the pot, turn it upside down, and as you place it on the ground, tuck your plant inside. After you have spread the mulch, pull off the pot and your precious little plant is nice and clean! In an area where you have several plugs, use smaller pots or plastic cups. My method is to cover about twelve to fifteen plants and shift to the next set of plants once the initial area is mulched. This seems to go a lot faster than trying to cover all the little ones beforehand.

Your planting may look more barren than you had anticipated, but don't be dismayed. Give it time. Remember that gardens grow, just like our souls.

You have arranged, planted, watered, and mulched. It is now time to place your designated object of prayer focus and bring your project to completion. In a memorial garden this object could be the dedication plaque. In a private garden it could be the birdbath, a rock, or the seating.

---

* Dark black mulch is highly discouraged in gardens that receive direct sunlight because it creates a heat sink (think of solar panels) that will destroy most plants' roots.

Whatever it is, now is the time to place it reverently in your personal sacred space.

Enjoy your garden. Use it. As you learn to find solace in your space, remember that you can come to a garden but not to garden. There will be times for tending your garden, both spiritually and physically.

In the next chapters, you will find gardening basics, written predominantly for the beginner. Then we move into part 2 the journal part of the book. If you are an experienced gardener, feel free to skip forward. Whether novice or veteran, as you begin tending your garden, begin also using the prayer journaling pages in chapter 18. This activity is an essential element for spiritual growth.

God's choicest blessings as all things grow.

14
Gardening Tools

Over the years your tool assortment will increase as your gardening needs change. The only advice on tool selection I'll offer is to buy a high quality bypass hand pruner (Felco™ brand, though expensive, really lasts; I've had mine for nearly fifty years) and a sharpener tool or honing stone.

With tools that have long handles, look for the collar to be bolted into the shaft and not merely clamped.

Knowing how to sharpen your tools properly is important, and is easily mastered. Look online for videos, contact your county extension office for a class, or ask that longtime–know-everything gardener to teach you.

1. Gloves

    - Cloth gloves offer little protection and are used mainly to keep hands clean. These can be laundered.
    - Rubber-coated gloves (coated fingers and palms) protect hands offering a barrier against sharp edges and allow flexibility and breathability. These are in my opinion a

good inexpensive solution for general gardening needs. These too can be laundered, but they must be air-dried. Fully rubberized gloves are hot, heavy, and used primarily when handling chemicals.
- Leather gloves are more expensive, offer the best protection for your hands, and are somewhat water-resistant. After use, brush off soil, and occasionally use saddle soap (applied as if washing your hands with gloves on) to keep the leather supple; avoid submerging leather gloves. If you grow roses, you'll want the protection leather offers. Some styles have leather palms and fingers with canvas backs.
- Pro tip: If you choose not to wear gloves, as when weeding or planting, and before you begin, scratch a bar of biodegradable soap, such as castile soap, so it gets under your fingernails.

2. Hat — When you'll be in the garden for several hours, use a full brim hat that has a vented crown for sun protection over scalp, neck, and ears. For briefer periods, use a visor style hat to shade your eyes.
3. Rubber tubs, plastic pail, or collapsible yard waste containers for debris
4. Hose with shower head watering wand (not a sprayer!)
5. Watering can with removable head
6. Carrier for small tools, which can also be a plastic pail
7. Hand pruners (secateurs) — Bypass pruners work like a knife for live stems; anvil pruners crush and are used for cutting dead wood.
8. Garden scissors
9. Hand trowel — There are nearly a dozen types of trowel blades available. Start with a traditional trowel having a wide blade with curved sides, and add a Dutch hand hoe (very multi-purpose!) or Hori Hori knife for rock gardening, weeding deep rooted weeds, and creating a trough for sowing seeds.

10. Hand cultivator, three-tined
11. Hand hoe

    - Traditional blade: square blade at nearly right angle to shaft
    - Dutch blade: sharpened crescent shaped blade sharply curved from the shaft

12. Hoe — A standard paddle or square edge is most common; a stirrup hoe cuts weeds just below the surface, disturbing the soil less.
13. Shovel — The usual large round blade shovel is used for digging large holes, and a smaller floral/perennial blade is used for smaller potted plant holes.
14. Edging spade — usually a squared straight edge blade used for cutting sod or creating trenches
15. Rake — There are several types for specific jobs; here are two basic ones to consider as a beginner:

    - A lawn/leaf rake has wide-spread long flexible tines for collecting debris, or narrow tines for getting into small spaces between plants.
    - A garden/bow rake has short, evenly spaced hard metal tines along a ridge at nearly a right angle to the shaft used for leveling or smoothing, gathering debris, and grooming turf.

16. Wheelbarrow or garden cart
17. Hedge shears or trimmers — excellent for cutting down ornamental grasses, among other uses
18. Loppers — large bypass pruners used for small woody limbs, often having extendable shafts
19. Hand saw — Folding (preferred) or bow, are used for larger caliper limbs.
20. Pro tip: Keep an inexpensive second folding hand saw for

use in the soil for cutting through roots too thick to cut with a spade.
21. Pitchfork — There are several for specific uses. Two of the most common for a gardener are:

    - A garden fork has four stiff thick tines for breaking up soil and usually a shorter shaft.
    - A compost fork has four to five long thin tines for lifting and stirring with a long shaft.

22. One gallon/3.8 liter pump sprayer: one for pesticides and another for herbicides, with each canister clearly marked!
23. Pro tip: Mark the bottom of the tank where the pressure hose touches, and when nearly empty, tip the canister to this point to use up the last of the solution.
24. Garden stakes: bamboo, metal, or fiberglass in varying lengths — purchase long bamboo stakes; you can cut them to length.
25. Twine or garden tape
26. Fertilizer, general all-purpose or specific (see chart on page 124)
27. Kneeler stand/seat, or knee pads

15
Gardening Techniques

READING A PLANT TAG

Most retailers sell plants with tags from the supplier/grower giving you information about the potted plant.

Besides the botanical name and general description of the appearance of the plant, specifics are provided and should include Hardiness Zone. They may also include bloom period, divisional needs, or pruning information. "How to Grow" information will include light requirements, water needs, height range, and average spread. The last bit of information, width, will indicate how far apart to place plants. You can use this information as you create your plant vocabulary chart mentioned in chapter 10, "Plant Selection."

HARDINESS ZONE

You will need to know what Hardiness Zone you live in. As discussed previously, a Hardiness Zone, whether addressing heat or cold, tells you that a plant grown in that area can endure a 50 percent kill-off of its root because of temperature and still survive.

You can create what is termed a *micro-climate* to slightly adjust a small portion of your garden to allow plants grown at the edge of their zone to survive. For example, to create a micro-climate in my zone 5 garden for a plant hardy in zone 6, I would grow it near the foundation of the house (warmer soil) on the leeward side (east and south), protected from winds and winter storms, and I would mulch heavily during the winter.

ANNUALS, PERENNIALS, AND BIENNIALS

Strictly defined, an *annual* is a plant whose entire life cycle, from initial seed, to growth and flower, to seed occurs in a single season and all vegetative parts — roots, stems, and leaves — die. Only the seeds carry over in each successive generation.

Perennials persist for generations by storage roots with the top vegetative portion of many perennials dying back each winter and growing back come the next season.

Biennials require two years to complete one life cycle. The first year from seed produces low-growing leaves. In the second year elongated vegetative growth results in flowers — and hence seeds — and then the mother plant dies. At the start of growing biennials it is suggested to replant in the second season. This is easily done from seeds; with nursery plants purchased while in bloom, do not deadhead, and allow seeds to develop and drop, or next season buy more potted plants in flower and interplant within last year's growth.

CALCULATING PLANTS

To know how many plants you will need to purchase for your garden, you first need to figure out how many square feet/centimeters there are. If your area is closer to a square or a rectangle, measure the length and the width of your space. Multiply the two together. If your area is similar to a circle, stretch a tape measure across the widest part of the circle, and then multiply it by 3.14.

Once you know how many square feet/centimeters you will be planting, you can figure out how many plants will fit in that area. The spacing information is on the plant's tag and tells you how far apart to plant each one. By using the chart below you will know how many plants to buy for each square foot/centimeter you've calculated.

This may seem excessive for a small garden when you are able to determine that you only need three or four plants. But for those of you working on larger, new, or public prayer gardens the spacing multiplier is invaluable.

Spacing Multiplier

This is a very simple procedure: Take the square feet/centimeters that you calculated and multiply it by the number in the second column, based on the spacing information for the plant in the first column.

Spacing between plants	Spacing multiplier; how many plants needed per sq. ft./cm
4" / 10 cm	9
5" / 13 cm	5.76
6" / 15 cm	4
7" / 18 cm	2.94
8" / 20 cm	2.25
9" / 23 cm	1.78
10" / 25 cm	1.45
11" / 28 cm	1.19
12" / 30 cm	1
15" / 38 cm	0.64
18" / 46 cm	0.44
24" / 61 cm	0.25
30" / 76 cm	0.16
36" / 91 cm	0.11

FROM POT TO GARDEN

The first rule of thumb for all potted plants is that the level of soil around the plant in the garden should be the same level as the soil in the pot. Planting something too high will expose its roots to air. It will also dry out the root ball more quickly. Plant too deeply and the stem, crown (the base of a perennial plant where the stems emerge), or trunk of the plant can rot from lack of air and sunlight.

The process for transplanting starts the night before with watering the pots. Plants take up and hold the largest percentage of water during the night. Your plants will be better able to withstand root disturbances that inhibit water intake during the day when the cells of the plant are turgid (already full of water). If you plan on planting them later in the day after the harshest sun has passed, then set the watered pots in a shaded location until then.

There is only a slight difference between planting herbaceous plants like perennials and annuals and planting hardwoods such as trees and shrubs. Research has shown that larger hardwoods need reused soil that was dug out to backfill the hole and they should not have the soil altered by amendments. Adding *mychorrizae* inoculants to enhance root development is fine and encouraged.

The reason for not enhancing the soil is because the root system is less likely to expand beyond the amended soil into harder, less nutrient-rich soil. This causes the roots to form a circular mass that will eventually fill the space, eliminating the necessary proportion of soil to root mass and creating a potential for girdling — the roots literally strangle themselves and ultimately kill the plant. It is always best to select the right plant for the site with its existing soil condition.

These are the steps for planting either herbaceous or hardwood plants:

1. Dig the hole twice as wide and 1½ times as deep as the container or root ball.
2. For herbaceous plants, amend the soil with compost.
3. Use enough soil to raise the bottom of the hole to the same height as the container or root ball. Remember, you want the

soil level of the container, pot, or root ball to be the same height as the hole when you're finished. For larger trees/shrubs, place a wooden joist across the hole to determine ground level.

4. Add *mychorrizae* inoculants to the bottom of the hole to enhance root development and mix with some of the removed soil.
5. Remove plants from their container or root ball wrap (yes, remove the burlap and wire that it was shipped in) and carefully loosen their roots. If the roots are severely entangled, or root-bound, you may need to make three or four minor cuts into the sides of the root mass near the bottom to be able to pull them slightly apart packing in garden soil between cuts.
6. Place the plant in the hole, spreading the roots evenly and adding a little water. Use a liquid transplant fertilizer, organic or commercial, at this point of watering. Again, be sure the plant will be at the same soil level.
7. Backfill the hole with soil, making sure you avoid air pockets. Pack it slightly with your hands as you go. Don't compact the soil by pressing it down really hard or stomping on it.
8. Build up the soil away from the central stem or crown. This forms a moat around the plant that will help contain water.
9. Water thoroughly. If you have transplanted a very large tree and the root ball seemed dry, leave the hose to drip water near the trunk for three or four hours to saturate it.
10. For larger trees, stake the trunk to prevent the tree from tipping during the first year while the root system expands. Use three stakes placed about three to four feet/one meter away from the trunk and evenly spaced around it. When the stakes are pounded into the ground they need to be at least one-half the height of the trunk. Run heavy gauge wire through sections of old hose.* Rest the wired hose against the trunk above the limb and secure each end of the wire to your stakes. Do not pull the wires too tight — you want to

---

* Staking kits are also available.

stabilize the tree, not choke it. You will check these supports throughout the year and adjust the tension as needed so as to not girdle the trunk as it grows.
11. Mulch the area up to the ridge of the moat. After your plant is established, you can level the moat and cover this area with mulch as well. Do not mound mulch like a volcano around hardwood trunks; doing so will rot the bark and suffocate the tree! Herbaceous plants are usually established in a few weeks. Hardwoods, especially larger trees, may take several months.

Transplanting

Transplanting is best done in the spring or, for trees and shrubs, early autumn. If you find that you will be transplanting during the summer, anticipate the need to protect your plants from excessive sunlight, heat, and wind until they are established enough to take up the necessary water (about ten to fourteen days for herbaceous plants).

A method I use involves rigging shade from white pillowcases and sheets picked up at yard sales or resale stores. The white fabric diffuses direct sunlight without creating excessive shade. For taller plants, drive posts into the ground so they will be about one-third higher than the plant on the sides where the sun and wind come from. Attach the fabric to the posts with safety pins or garden wire to form a wall. For plants that are very short, place a single layer of white fabric on top before the hottest part of the day, and secure with handfuls of mulch or small rocks. Be sure to pull back the material in the early evening to allow the plants to breathe during the night and the early morning hours.

Planting under Trees

First, you may need to improve the soil. If you do, take care not to harm the tree's roots or trunk. After all, it is the tree that you appreciate and want to flourish.

The procedure of improving the soil will take a few years (about two or three) before you can make your final planting. Using containers until that time lets you make use of the space until you can plant your garden permanently around the tree.

Remember that trees are heavy feeders and big drinkers. Even with soil conditioning, your garden under their limbs will need special consideration with regard to planning, plant selection, water, and fertilizing.

You can enrich the soil with thoroughly composted organic matter and leaves. The tree already provides the biggest part of the conditioning material needed. Gather the leaves and chop them into small pieces using a yard chopper or bagging-style lawn mower. Combine the organic matter and leaves and spread it under the tree at no more than four inches/ten centimeters deep per season. Be sure to stay about six to eight inches/fifteen to twenty centimeters away from the trunk. Sprinkle with a little compost activator, or use finely chopped yarrow (*Achillea millefolium* cvs) clippings, and water the area. Keep this area moist (but not waterlogged) until winter.

Mow down any weeds that may take root, being careful not to damage any tree-knees — those roots exposed on the surface. Pile on the next round of chopped leaves the following autumn.

Repeat this procedure one more time (the third autumn), adding enough compost to create a raised bed eight to ten inches/twenty to twenty-five centimeters at the outer edge to less than one inch/two and half centimeters near the trunk. Do not build up compost around the tree trunk. The skirt at the base of the tree, that section at ground level that flares out from the vertical trunk, should be exposed to air movement. Now let the "earthworks," as I have named them, (microbes, worms, and bugs) move in and loosen the composted soil for you. By the third summer you should have a nice, soft, friable soil and it will be possible to plant your shade garden under the boughs of your beautiful tree.

16
Composting

Compost is considered black gold, a perfect amendment to loosen soils and to add nutrients. In my previous book, *A Catholic Gardener's Spiritual Almanac*, I wrote the following about composting and here it bears repeating:

> When it came to composting, I was initially a reluctant participant. In several gardening circles I would hear others talk about their compost piles as of a special pet: feeding it greens, keeping it warm, and never adding junk food to its microbial digestion. My eyes would glaze over as temperatures and techniques were debated. There were several misconceptions I had to resolve before I could really embrace this activity.*

Listed here are some of the misconceptions explained. A Compost Rotation Chart is included at the back of the book, chapter 23.

COMPOSTING IS COMPLICATED

Those who are into composting are, well, into it. They have read articles

---

* Margaret Rose Realy, *A Catholic Gardener's Spiritual Almanac* (Ave Maria Press, 2015), 80.

and books gleaning information, but you needn't worry about all that. Pile whatever composting materials you have and it will decompose; as the saying goes, compost happens. Now and then, turning it over and adding water will speed the process. If you tend to forget about your pile, as I often do, nature will still run its course, less efficiently but none the less.

THE YARD IS TOO SMALL FOR A COMPOST PILE

Think of it this way: If you have a large yard your compost pile is usually larger; with a small yard the pile will be smaller in proportion. If you have a small garden, use a large thirty-two- to thirty-nine-gallon black plastic garbage can with a tight-fitting lid. Drill half-inch holes around its sides and bottom for air movement. To stir the compost, add a little water, lay the container on its side — with lid secured by bungee cords hooked into the drilled holes — and roll it around.

COMPOST PILES STINK AND ATTRACT RODENTS

Most people have this misconception. Compost piles do not attract rodents or have a bad odor unless the wrong stuff is added. The general rule here is no animal products: meats and bones, oils, dairy, eggs, or poo. Do not add sugary materials either. Add only vegetative materials from the kitchen or yard. Healthy compost smells like spring soil.

COMPOST PILES ARE UGLY

Location is everything. Placing it in the middle of the yard or driveway will certainly create an eyesore. Locate it in an out-of-the-way place where it will receive a lot of sunlight. You can hide the pile by using fence panels or, again, by using black garbage cans. There are also commercial composting containers, tumblers, and bins available on the market.

I DON'T HAVE THE TIME TO COMPOST

This was a favorite myth of mine. I believed I was far too busy to focus on creating the healthy compost pile that gardeners bragged about. Once my compost pile was started, I discovered it took less than twenty minutes a month to flip the pile and maintain it.

17
Fertilizer

What does N-P-K on a bag of fertilizer apply to? Here is a little memory aid that I created and use as a handout. Folks who are not experienced gardeners found it helpful in remembering the codes on the packaging:

N= **N**itrogen = **N**ice Leaves
P= **Ph**osphorous = **Ph**lowers and **Ph**ruit
K= Potassium* = that which you **K**eep covered, as in the roots

Now when you look at the analysis on the package of a fertilizer you will have a better understanding of what each number means in relation to your plants. See the chart on the next page for more details on specific fertilizer types.

A Soil Amendment chart is included in chapter 20.

---

* The chemical symbol for potassium, *K*, comes from *kalium*, Latin for potash, derived from the Arabic *qali*, meaning alkali. Potassium is a member of the alkali group of the periodic table.

Fertilizer and Amendment Chart*

Name	Form	Type	Main Nutrients	Additional Nutrients
Bat guano	Powder, granule	Organic	Nitrogen, phosphorus	Macro and micronutrients
Blood meal	Powder	Organic	Nitrogen	
Bone meal	Powder	Organic	Phosphorous	Nitrogen
Bulb food	Powder	Inorganic	Phosphorous	Nitrogen, potassium
Dolomite lime	Powder	Inorganic	Calcium	Magnesium, also raises pH
Fish emulsion	Liquid	Organic	Nitrogen	Phosphorus, potassium
Greensand	Powder, granule	Organic	Potassium	Magnesium, micronutrients
Liquid seaweed	Liquid	Organic	Potassium	Nitrogen, micronutrients, trace elements
Magnesium sulfate	Powder	Inorganic	Sulfur, magnesium	

---

* This information was expanded upon from the chart in McGee and Stucky's *The Bountiful Container*, p. 69.

Mushroom compost	Granule	Organic		Macro and micronutrients, trace elements
Rock phosphate	Powder	Organic	Phosphorus	Micronutrients, calcium
Super-phosphate	Powder	Inorganic	Phosphorus	Sulfur
Worm castings	Powder, granule	Organic	Nitrogen	Calcium, micronutrients

PART 2
Continuing to Grow

18
Prayer Garden Journaling

*Help us to be ever faithful gardeners of the spirit,
who know that without darkness nothing comes
to birth, and without light nothing flowers.*

— Mary Sarton

A journal is a means of simply tracking what is going on — a list, if you will. Journaling, on the other hand, is an exploration of what you *perceive* and how it affects your perceptions. In this portion of the book you have a section for both, a garden journal and spiritual journaling. The focus now is on continued gardening success and spiritual growth as you continue gardening and praying in your sacred outdoor space.

The portion that is the garden journal will help you chart and keep track of diseases and growth, and the included prayer journaling section will help you keep track of spiritual weaknesses and spiritual developments.

This is followed by the worksheets for tracking what is happening in the garden, and will enhance the knowledge of gardening for both the experienced gardener and the novice. While this book includes only one year's worth of journal space, ideally you will journal in your garden every year. The book is designed so that you can photocopy the pages and add them to the binder you created in Part 1. Don't give up — if you continue learning, trying, and journaling for about four years, you will have an excellent mastery of the garden.

PRAYER JOURNALING

> *A beginner must think of herself as one setting out to make a garden in which her Beloved Lord is to take his delight.*
> — Saint Teresa of Avila[*]

Prayer is personal; it is a conversation with the Persons of the triune God. Some of you prefer the discovery, or the familiarity of, a memorized prayer that touches your heart; others (like me) get rather casual in prayerful conversations, as if talking with a dear friend. Whatever your style, if it draws you into a closer relationship with all that is holy, follow it.

Learning to perceive God in the garden, to listen to what the Holy Spirit may be offering, is new for some of you. Here is a guideline to help you develop this listening during your prayer time. You may find as you journey through your days that the Holy Spirit will prompt you to listen to nature at unexpected moments outside of your garden.

To begin, the Creator is visible in his creation. In the very first paragraph of the prologue to the Catechism of the Catholic Church we read, "at every time and in every place God draws closer to man." The Catechism clearly states that through the "world's order and beauty, one can come to a knowledge of God. … Ever since the creation of the world his invisible nature, namely his eternal power and deity, has been clearly perceived in things that have been made. … Their beauty is a profession" (CCC 32).

When beginning to journal with nature, two approaches work best. **Narrative** — writing about an experience where you learned something about yourself; this type of writing:

---

[*] Teresa of Avila, *The Book of My Life, Part Two, The Four Waters*. There are many translations available of Saint Teresa's writings.

- Tells a story, whether an imaginative exploration or personal experience,
- Sets up the narrative background and theme,
- Describes and develop the metaphor and then finishes it by expressing the point.

Descriptive — describing an object that has sentimental value to you. You might include:

- introductory description of the sensory object,
- personal impressions of it,
- analogies and conclusion.

Neither style asks *why* a particular object (flora, fauna, or earth) created the reflection, but rather *how* a particular object influenced a spiritual connection. We strive to find God and an expression of his goodness nestled in the womb of wilderness.

To help develop your listening skills, think of the activity as a *lectio divina* with nature. *Lectio divina* is a practice of reading scripture with attention to the promptings of the Holy Spirit – that means noticing when a word or verse or phrase jumps out at you and then lingering with it, to discover what God wants to teach you. This promotes communion with God and increases knowledge of the Word — scripture not simply as mere text, but as the word, personal and personally relevant. Bringing this practice into a reading of creation also promotes communion with God and increases awareness of God's presence all around us, and this method of prayer also becomes surprisingly personal.

The parallels of this reading (especially key for development of metaphors) are:

- First, perceive the word, or for our purposes, the planting or element of nature.
- Then, meditate and contemplate on what has sparked spiritual movement.

- Last, communicate what the Holy Spirit has helped you experience.

The practice of *lectio divina* helps us to become less distracted, less chaotic through the process of slowing down to read the Word (or creation) and then to perceive God's intention for you in the study.

By teaching yourself to see in this new way, we can experience the beauty and wonder of God expressed through nature. The steady practice of *lectio* can, eventually, help us to better see everything, and everyone, put before us.

Initially it may be easier to look for a metaphor for what you are feeling: burdened, abundant in gratitude, anxious in anticipation or waiting. Through practice you will grow into openness – just like a blooming flower – and become more and more able to recognize the Holy Spirit's movement, absorbing its lessons to develop a spiritual narrative.

From Isaiah 45:18 we read of our God, the maker of the earth who established it not as an empty waste, but a thing to be lived in. He willed for us to live in the awareness of his presence through his creation and not waste experiencing one of his many forms of love.

Apply the practices mentioned above in the journaling pages that follow.

WEEKLY STEPS FOR SUCCESS: USING THE GARDEN JOURNAL PAGES

As a reminder, since the following journal pages are for only one year of tracking you are free to copy these pages to add to your garden notebook.

The prayer focus for the week can be whatever advancement you would like to make spiritually, a list of folks to pray for, or personal intentions.

The first set of pages are titled Weather Journal. It is on these pages you'll keep track of the climate. Write the season you're noting – such as spring or autumn – and what your goal might be for that week of gardening.

Temperature will be the high/low for that day. Next is rainfall, if any, followed by wind speed that can be such as mild, none, or gale force or tracked by using a weather app with a predicted wind speed in MPH. The Celestial Sphere is simply cloudy, overcast, or clear.

Weekly Steps for Success

Season: _____
Garden Goal: _____
Weather Journal

Week of:	M	T	W	R	F	S	U
Temperature high/low							
Rainfall							
Winds							
Celestial Sphere*							

PRAYER FOCUS

_____
_____
_____
_____
_____
_____
_____

* (i.e., sunny, level of cloudiness, pollution)

Season: _____
Garden Goal: _____
Weather Journal

Week of:	M	T	W	R	F	S	U
Temperature high/low							
Rainfall							
Winds							
Celestial Sphere*							

PRAYER FOCUS

_____
_____
_____
_____
_____
_____
_____
_____
_____
_____

Season: _____
Garden Goal: _____
Weather Journal

Week of:	M	T	W	R	F	S	U
Temperature high/low							
Rainfall							
Winds							
Celestial Sphere*							

PRAYER FOCUS

_____
_____
_____
_____
_____
_____
_____
_____
_____
_____

Season: _____
Garden Goal: _____
Weather Journal

Week of:	M	T	W	R	F	S	U
Temperature high/low							
Rainfall							
Winds							
Celestial Sphere*							

PRAYER FOCUS

_____
_____
_____
_____
_____
_____
_____
_____
_____

Season: _____
Garden Goal: _____
Weather Journal

Week of:	M	T	W	R	F	S	U
Temperature high/low							
Rainfall							
Winds							
Celestial Sphere*							

PRAYER FOCUS

_____
_____
_____
_____
_____
_____
_____
_____
_____
_____

Season: _____
Garden Goal: _____
Weather Journal

Week of:	M	T	W	R	F	S	U
Temperature high/low							
Rainfall							
Winds							
Celestial Sphere*							

PRAYER FOCUS

_____
_____
_____
_____
_____
_____
_____
_____
_____

Season: _____
Garden Goal: _____
Weather Journal

Week of:	M	T	W	R	F	S	U
Temperature high/low							
Rainfall							
Winds							
Celestial Sphere*							

PRAYER FOCUS

Season: _____
Garden Goal: _____
Weather Journal

Week of:	M	T	W	R	F	S	U
Temperature high/low							
Rainfall							
Winds							
Celestial Sphere*							

PRAYER FOCUS

_____
_____
_____
_____
_____
_____
_____
_____
_____

Season: _____
Garden Goal: _____
Weather Journal

Week of:	M	T	W	R	F	S	U
Temperature high/low							
Rainfall							
Winds							
Celestial Sphere*							

PRAYER FOCUS

_____
_____
_____
_____
_____
_____
_____
_____
_____

Season: _____
Garden Goal: _____
Weather Journal

Week of:	M	T	W	R	F	S	U
Temperature high/low							
Rainfall							
Winds							
Celestial Sphere*							

PRAYER FOCUS

_____
_____
_____
_____
_____
_____
_____
_____
_____
_____

Season: _____
Garden Goal: _____
Weather Journal

Week of:	M	T	W	R	F	S	U
Temperature high/low							
Rainfall							
Winds							
Celestial Sphere*							

PRAYER FOCUS

_____
_____
_____
_____
_____
_____
_____
_____
_____

Season: _____
Garden Goal: _____
Weather Journal

Week of:	M	T	W	R	F	S	U
Temperature high/low							
Rainfall							
Winds							
Celestial Sphere*							

PRAYER FOCUS

_____
_____
_____
_____
_____
_____
_____
_____
_____
_____

146 *Weekly Steps for Success*

Season: _____
Garden Goal: _____
Weather Journal

Week of:	M	T	W	R	F	S	U
Temperature high/low							
Rainfall							
Winds							
Celestial Sphere*							

PRAYER FOCUS

_____
_____
_____
_____
_____
_____
_____
_____
_____
_____

Season: _____
Garden Goal: _____
Weather Journal

Week of:	M	T	W	R	F	S	U
Temperature high/low							
Rainfall							
Winds							
Celestial Sphere*							

PRAYER FOCUS

Season: _____
Garden Goal: _____
Weather Journal

Week of:	M	T	W	R	F	S	U
Temperature high/low							
Rainfall							
Winds							
Celestial Sphere*							

PRAYER FOCUS

Season: _____
Garden Goal: _____
Weather Journal

Week of:	M	T	W	R	F	S	U
Temperature high/low							
Rainfall							
Winds							
Celestial Sphere*							

PRAYER FOCUS

_____
_____
_____
_____
_____
_____
_____
_____
_____

Season: _____
Garden Goal: _____
Weather Journal

Week of:	M	T	W	R	F	S	U
Temperature high/low							
Rainfall							
Winds							
Celestial Sphere*							

PRAYER FOCUS

_____
_____
_____
_____
_____
_____
_____
_____
_____
_____

Weekly Steps for Success **151**

Season: _____
Garden Goal: _____
Weather Journal

Week of:	M	T	W	R	F	S	U
Temperature high/low							
Rainfall							
Winds							
* Celestial Sphere*							

PRAYER FOCUS

_____
_____
_____
_____
_____
_____
_____
_____
_____

Season: _____
Garden Goal: _____
Weather Journal

Week of:	M	T	W	R	F	S	U
Temperature high/low							
Rainfall							
Winds							
Celestial Sphere*							

PRAYER FOCUS

_____
_____
_____
_____
_____
_____
_____
_____
_____
_____

Season: _____
Garden Goal: _____
Weather Journal

Week of:	M	T	W	R	F	S	U
Temperature high/low							
Rainfall							
Winds							
Celestial Sphere*							

PRAYER FOCUS

_____
_____
_____
_____
_____
_____
_____
_____
_____

Season: _____
Garden Goal: _____
Weather Journal

Week of:	M	T	W	R	F	S	U
Temperature high/low							
Rainfall							
Winds							
Celestial Sphere*							

PRAYER FOCUS

_____

_____

_____

_____

_____

_____

_____

_____

_____

_____

Weekly Steps for Success **155**

Season: _____
Garden Goal: _____
Weather Journal

Week of:	M	T	W	R	F	S	U
Temperature high/low							
Rainfall							
Winds							
Celestial Sphere*							

PRAYER FOCUS

_____
_____
_____
_____
_____
_____
_____
_____
_____

Season: _____
Garden Goal: _____
Weather Journal

Week of:	M	T	W	R	F	S	U
Temperature high/low							
Rainfall							
Winds							
Celestial Sphere*							

PRAYER FOCUS

_____
_____
_____
_____
_____
_____
_____
_____
_____
_____

Season: _____
Garden Goal: _____
Weather Journal

Week of:	M	T	W	R	F	S	U
Temperature high/low							
Rainfall							
Winds							
Celestial Sphere*							

PRAYER FOCUS

_____
_____
_____
_____
_____
_____
_____
_____
_____

158 Weekly Steps for Success

Season: _____
Garden Goal: _____
Weather Journal

Week of:	M	T	W	R	F	S	U
Temperature high/low							
Rainfall							
Winds							
Celestial Sphere*							

PRAYER FOCUS

_____
_____
_____
_____
_____
_____
_____
_____
_____

Weekly Steps for Success **159**

Season: _____
Garden Goal: _____
Weather Journal

Week of:	M	T	W	R	F	S	U
Temperature high/low							
Rainfall							
Winds							
Celestial Sphere*							

PRAYER FOCUS

_____
_____
_____
_____
_____
_____
_____
_____
_____

Season: _____
Garden Goal: _____
Weather Journal

Week of:	M	T	W	R	F	S	U
Temperature high/low							
Rainfall							
Winds							
Celestial Sphere*							

PRAYER FOCUS

_____
_____
_____
_____
_____
_____
_____
_____
_____
_____

Season: _____
Garden Goal: _____
Weather Journal

Week of:	M	T	W	R	F	S	U
Temperature high/low							
Rainfall							
Winds							
Celestial Sphere*							

PRAYER FOCUS

_____
_____
_____
_____
_____
_____
_____
_____
_____

Weekly Steps for Success

Season: _____
Garden Goal: _____
Weather Journal

Week of:	M	T	W	R	F	S	U
Temperature high/low							
Rainfall							
Winds							
Celestial Sphere*							

PRAYER FOCUS

_____
_____
_____
_____
_____
_____
_____
_____
_____
_____

Weekly Steps for Success **163**

Season: _____
Garden Goal: _____
Weather Journal

Week of:	M	T	W	R	F	S	U
Temperature high/low							
Rainfall							
Winds							
Celestial Sphere*							

PRAYER FOCUS

_____
_____
_____
_____
_____
_____
_____
_____
_____

164 *Weekly Steps for Success*

Season: _____
Garden Goal: _____
Weather Journal

Week of:	M	T	W	R	F	S	U
Temperature high/low							
Rainfall							
Winds							
Celestial Sphere*							

PRAYER FOCUS

_____
_____
_____
_____
_____
_____
_____
_____
_____

Season: _____
Garden Goal: _____
Weather Journal

Week of:	M	T	W	R	F	S	U
Temperature high/low							
Rainfall							
Winds							
Celestial Sphere*							

PRAYER FOCUS

_____
_____
_____
_____
_____
_____
_____
_____
_____

166 *Weekly Steps for Success*

Season: _____
Garden Goal: _____
Weather Journal

Week of:	M	T	W	R	F	S	U
Temperature high/low							
Rainfall							
Winds							
Celestial Sphere*							

PRAYER FOCUS

_____
_____
_____
_____
_____
_____
_____
_____
_____

Weekly Steps for Success **167**

Season: _____
Garden Goal: _____
Weather Journal

Week of:	M	T	W	R	F	S	U
Temperature high/low							
Rainfall							
Winds							
Celestial Sphere*							

PRAYER FOCUS

_____
_____
_____
_____
_____
_____
_____
_____

Season: _____
Garden Goal: _____
Weather Journal

Week of:	M	T	W	R	F	S	U
Temperature high/low							
Rainfall							
Winds							
Celestial Sphere*							

PRAYER FOCUS

_____
_____
_____
_____
_____
_____
_____
_____
_____
_____

Season: _____
Garden Goal: _____
Weather Journal

Week of:	M	T	W	R	F	S	U
Temperature high/low							
Rainfall							
Winds							
Celestial Sphere*							

PRAYER FOCUS

_____
_____
_____
_____
_____
_____
_____
_____
_____
_____

Season: _____
Garden Goal: _____
Weather Journal

Week of:	M	T	W	R	F	S	U
Temperature high/low							
Rainfall							
Winds							
Celestial Sphere*							

PRAYER FOCUS

_____
_____
_____
_____
_____
_____
_____
_____
_____

Season: _____
Garden Goal: _____
Weather Journal

Week of:	M	T	W	R	F	S	U
Temperature high/low							
Rainfall							
Winds							
Celestial Sphere*							

PRAYER FOCUS

_____
_____
_____
_____
_____
_____
_____
_____

Season: _____
Garden Goal: _____
Weather Journal

Week of:	M	T	W	R	F	S	U
Temperature high/low							
Rainfall							
Winds							
Celestial Sphere*							

PRAYER FOCUS

_____
_____
_____
_____
_____
_____
_____
_____
_____

Season: _____
Garden Goal: _____
Weather Journal

Week of:	M	T	W	R	F	S	U
Temperature high/low							
Rainfall							
Winds							
Celestial Sphere*							

PRAYER FOCUS

_____
_____
_____
_____
_____
_____
_____
_____
_____

Season: _____
Garden Goal: _____
Weather Journal

Week of:	M	T	W	R	F	S	U
Temperature high/low							
Rainfall							
Winds							
Celestial Sphere*							

PRAYER FOCUS

_____
_____
_____
_____
_____
_____
_____
_____
_____

Season: _____
Garden Goal: _____
Weather Journal

Week of:	M	T	W	R	F	S	U
Temperature high/low							
Rainfall							
Winds							
Celestial Sphere*							

PRAYER FOCUS

_____
_____
_____
_____
_____
_____
_____
_____
_____

Season: _____
Garden Goal: _____
Weather Journal

Week of:	M	T	W	R	F	S	U
Temperature high/low							
Rainfall							
Winds							
Celestial Sphere*							

PRAYER FOCUS

_____
_____
_____
_____
_____
_____
_____
_____
_____
_____

Season: _____

Garden Goal: _____

Weather Journal

Week of:	M	T	W	R	F	S	U
Temperature high/low							
Rainfall							
Winds							
Celestial Sphere*							

PRAYER FOCUS

_____
_____
_____
_____
_____
_____
_____
_____
_____

Season: _____
Garden Goal: _____
Weather Journal

Week of:	M	T	W	R	F	S	U
Temperature high/low							
Rainfall							
Winds							
Celestial Sphere*							

PRAYER FOCUS

_____
_____
_____
_____
_____
_____
_____
_____
_____

Season: _____

Garden Goal: _____

Weather Journal

Week of:	M	T	W	R	F	S	U
Temperature high/low							
Rainfall							
Winds							
Celestial Sphere*							

PRAYER FOCUS

_____
_____
_____
_____
_____
_____
_____
_____
_____
_____

Season: _____
Garden Goal: _____
Weather Journal

Week of:	M	T	W	R	F	S	U
Temperature high/low							
Rainfall							
Winds							
Celestial Sphere*							

PRAYER FOCUS

_____
_____
_____
_____
_____
_____
_____
_____
_____
_____

Season: _____
Garden Goal: _____
Weather Journal

Week of:	M	T	W	R	F	S	U
Temperature high/low							
Rainfall							
Winds							
Celestial Sphere*							

PRAYER FOCUS

_____
_____
_____
_____
_____
_____
_____
_____
_____

Season: _____
Garden Goal: _____
Weather Journal

Week of:	M	T	W	R	F	S	U
Temperature high/low							
Rainfall							
Winds							
Celestial Sphere*							

PRAYER FOCUS

_____
_____
_____
_____
_____
_____
_____
_____
_____
_____

Season: _____
Garden Goal: _____
Weather Journal

Week of:	M	T	W	R	F	S	U
Temperature high/low							
Rainfall							
Winds							
Celestial Sphere*							

PRAYER FOCUS

_____
_____
_____
_____
_____
_____
_____
_____
_____
_____

Season: _____
Garden Goal: _____
Weather Journal

Week of:	M	T	W	R	F	S	U
Temperature high/low							
Rainfall							
Winds							
Celestial Sphere*							

PRAYER FOCUS

_____
_____
_____
_____
_____
_____
_____
_____
_____

Season: _____
Garden Goal: _____
Weather Journal

Week of:	M	T	W	R	F	S	U
Temperature high/low							
Rainfall							
Winds							
Celestial Sphere*							

PRAYER FOCUS

_____
_____
_____
_____
_____
_____
_____
_____
_____
_____

Season: _____
Garden Goal: _____
Weather Journal

Week of:	M	T	W	R	F	S	U
Temperature high/low							
Rainfall							
Winds							
Celestial Sphere*							

PRAYER FOCUS

_____
_____
_____
_____
_____
_____
_____
_____
_____

Season: _____
Garden Goal: _____
Weather Journal

Week of:	M	T	W	R	F	S	U
Temperature high/low							
Rainfall							
Winds							
Celestial Sphere*							

PRAYER FOCUS

_____
_____
_____
_____
_____
_____
_____
_____
_____
_____

Season: _____
Garden Goal: _____
Weather Journal

Week of:	M	T	W	R	F	S	U
Temperature high/low							
Rainfall							
Winds							
Celestial Sphere*							

PRAYER FOCUS

_____
_____
_____
_____
_____
_____
_____
_____
_____

Season: _____
Garden Goal: _____
Weather Journal

Week of:	M	T	W	R	F	S	U
Temperature high/low							
Rainfall							
Winds							
Celestial Sphere*							

PRAYER FOCUS

Season: _____
Garden Goal: _____
Weather Journal

Week of:	M	T	W	R	F	S	U
Temperature high/low							
Rainfall							
Winds							
Celestial Sphere*							

PRAYER FOCUS

Season: _____
Garden Goal: _____
Weather Journal

Week of:	M	T	W	R	F	S	U
Temperature high/low							
Rainfall							
Winds							
Celestial Sphere*							

PRAYER FOCUS

_____
_____
_____
_____
_____
_____
_____
_____
_____

Season: _____
Garden Goal: _____
Weather Journal

Week of:	M	T	W	R	F	S	U
Temperature high/low							
Rainfall							
Winds							
Celestial Sphere*							

PRAYER FOCUS

_____
_____
_____
_____
_____
_____
_____
_____
_____
_____

Season: _____
Garden Goal: _____
Weather Journal

Week of:	M	T	W	R	F	S	U
Temperature high/low							
Rainfall							
Winds							
Celestial Sphere*							

PRAYER FOCUS

_____
_____
_____
_____
_____
_____
_____
_____
_____

Season: _____
Garden Goal: _____
Weather Journal

Week of:	M	T	W	R	F	S	U
Temperature high/low							
Rainfall							
Winds							
Celestial Sphere*							

PRAYER FOCUS

_____
_____
_____
_____
_____
_____
_____
_____
_____
_____

Season: _____
Garden Goal: _____
Weather Journal

Week of:	M	T	W	R	F	S	U
Temperature high/low							
Rainfall							
Winds							
Celestial Sphere*							

PRAYER FOCUS

_____
_____
_____
_____
_____
_____
_____
_____
_____
_____

Season: _____
Garden Goal: _____
Weather Journal

Week of:	M	T	W	R	F	S	U
Temperature high/low							
Rainfall							
Winds							
Celestial Sphere*							

PRAYER FOCUS

Season: _____
Garden Goal: _____
Weather Journal

Week of:	M	T	W	R	F	S	U
Temperature high/low							
Rainfall							
Winds							
Celestial Sphere*							

PRAYER FOCUS

_____
_____
_____
_____
_____
_____
_____
_____
_____

19
Tracking Sunlight and Shade

This form is used when you plan to establish a new garden to determine plant selection. It is also helpful as a garden with trees matures, altering the amount of sunlight, and the garden needs to be revamped to account for the increasing shade.

Note which garden and check the amount of light at that time. You will do this once for each season.

Tracking Sunlight and Shade

Garden: _____		Season: _____		Garden: _____		Season: _____	
Time	Full sun	Part shade	Full shade	Time	Full sun	Part shade	Full shade
5 am				5 am			
6				6			
7				7			
8				8			
9				9			
10				10			
11				11			
12				12			
1 pm				1 pm			
2				2			
3				3			
4				4			
5				5			
6				6			
7				7			
8				8			
9				9			

Tracking Sunlight and Shade

Garden:_____ Season:_____ | Garden:_____ Season:_____

Time	Full sun	Part shade	Full shade	Time	Full sun	Part shade	Full shade
5 am				5 am			
6				6			
7				7			
8				8			
9				9			
10				10			
11				11			
12				12			
1 pm				1 pm			
2				2			
3				3			
4				4			
5				5			
6				6			
7				7			
8				8			
9				9			

20
Soil Amendments

This too is a chart that will only be used once at the onset of planning a garden, but is an essential part for any garden installation. Chapter 6, the section titled Soil, addresses assessing the soil, and here you will add that information and what amendments will need to be added.

Garden zone	Soil type (composition)	Amendment needed	Product added	Date

Soil Amendments

Garden zone	Soil type (composition)	Amendment needed	Product added	Date

21
Watering Needs/Schedule

Watering is more intuitive than a strict science unless you're producing marketable crops. If it's hot, windy, or dry you'll need to water more frequently per week. This chart will help you get used to the rhythm of your gardens' watering needs whether you're in an arid region or a costal area with lots of rain.

Watering Needs/Schedule

Plant or garden area	Date	Amount needed per week	Minus amount of rainfall	Supple-mental watering date

Plant or garden area	Date	Amount needed per week	Minus amount of rainfall	Supple-mental watering date

22
Tracking Diseases, Pests, and Weeds

Keeping track of the health of a garden, like our own spiritual health with journaling, is imperative for flourishing.

Copy this form for your garden notebook as you will use it often over the next few years.

Write what plants are affected and/or the garden area and the date – which will help you in following growing seasons as a possible preventative action.

212 Tracking Diseases, Pests, and Weeds

Plant or garden affected	Date	Pest

Disease	Weed	Solution

23
Compost Rotation Chart

This chart will help you get in the rhythm of tending to your compost pile. For many gardeners, the compost heap gets added to for a few weeks before the first turning. Simply note when you began the pile and move on from there.

Compost start date	First turning date	Second turning	Sifted and ready

Compost start date	First turning date	Second turning	Sifted and ready

24
Plant Selection and History

If you like record keeping of your plants, as I do, this information can grow exponentially over the years! This is the main portion of a garden notebook. We have provided several pages here, but do copy this form for your own notebook. Also create an index for locating plant information when needed.

Plant Selection and History

• • •

Common name _____

Botanical name _____

Christian symbolism _____

Where and when purchased _____

Date planted _____ Date seeds/cuttings started _____

Watering needs _____

Garden location_____

Bloom time and color _____

Fruiting time and yield _____

Pests or diseases _____

• • •

Common name _____

Botanical name _____

Christian symbolism _____

Where and when purchased _____

Date planted _____ Date seeds/cuttings started _____

Watering needs _____

Garden location_____

Bloom time and color _____

Fruiting time and yield _____

Pests or diseases _____

Plant Selection and History

• • •

Common name _____

Botanical name _____

Christian symbolism _____

Where and when purchased _____

Date planted _____ Date seeds/cuttings started _____

Watering needs _____

Garden location _____

Bloom time and color _____

Fruiting time and yield _____

Pests or diseases _____

• • •

Common name _____

Botanical name _____

Christian symbolism _____

Where and when purchased _____

Date planted _____ Date seeds/cuttings started _____

Watering needs _____

Garden location _____

Bloom time and color _____

Fruiting time and yield _____

Pests or diseases _____

• • •

Common name _____

Botanical name _____

Christian symbolism _____

Where and when purchased _____

Date planted _____ Date seeds/cuttings started _____

Watering needs _____

Garden location_____

Bloom time and color _____

Fruiting time and yield _____

Pests or diseases _____

• • •

Common name _____

Botanical name _____

Christian symbolism _____

Where and when purchased _____

Date planted _____ Date seeds/cuttings started _____

Watering needs _____

Garden location_____

Bloom time and color _____

Fruiting time and yield _____

Pests or diseases _____

• • •

Common name _____

Botanical name _____

Christian symbolism _____

Where and when purchased _____

Date planted _____ Date seeds/cuttings started _____

Watering needs _____

Garden location_____

Bloom time and color _____

Fruiting time and yield _____

Pests or diseases _____

• • •

Common name _____

Botanical name _____

Christian symbolism _____

Where and when purchased _____

Date planted _____ Date seeds/cuttings started _____

Watering needs _____

Garden location_____

Bloom time and color _____

Fruiting time and yield _____

Pests or diseases _____

Plant Selection and History

∙ ∙ ∙

Common name _____

Botanical name _____

Christian symbolism _____

Where and when purchased _____

Date planted _____ Date seeds/cuttings started _____

Watering needs _____

Garden location_____

Bloom time and color _____

Fruiting time and yield _____

Pests or diseases _____

∙ ∙ ∙

Common name _____

Botanical name _____

Christian symbolism _____

Where and when purchased _____

Date planted _____ Date seeds/cuttings started _____

Watering needs _____

Garden location_____

Bloom time and color _____

Fruiting time and yield _____

Pests or diseases _____

⋯

Common name _____

Botanical name _____

Christian symbolism _____

Where and when purchased _____

Date planted _____ Date seeds/cuttings started _____

Watering needs _____

Garden location_____

Bloom time and color _____

Fruiting time and yield _____

Pests or diseases _____

⋯

Common name _____

Botanical name _____

Christian symbolism _____

Where and when purchased _____

Date planted _____ Date seeds/cuttings started _____

Watering needs _____

Garden location_____

Bloom time and color _____

Fruiting time and yield _____

Pests or diseases _____

• • •

Common name _____

Botanical name _____

Christian symbolism _____

Where and when purchased _____

Date planted _____ Date seeds/cuttings started _____

Watering needs _____

Garden location_____

Bloom time and color _____

Fruiting time and yield _____

Pests or diseases _____

• • •

Common name _____

Botanical name _____

Christian symbolism _____

Where and when purchased _____

Date planted _____ Date seeds/cuttings started _____

Watering needs _____

Garden location_____

Bloom time and color _____

Fruiting time and yield _____

Pests or diseases _____

• • •

Common name _____

Botanical name _____

Christian symbolism _____

Where and when purchased _____

Date planted _____ Date seeds/cuttings started _____

Watering needs _____

Garden location_____

Bloom time and color _____

Fruiting time and yield _____

Pests or diseases _____

• • •

Common name _____

Botanical name _____

Christian symbolism _____

Where and when purchased _____

Date planted _____ Date seeds/cuttings started _____

Watering needs _____

Garden location_____

Bloom time and color _____

Fruiting time and yield _____

Pests or diseases _____

228 *Plant Selection and History*

• • •

Common name _____

Botanical name _____

Christian symbolism _____

Where and when purchased _____

Date planted _____ Date seeds/cuttings started _____

Watering needs _____

Garden location_____

Bloom time and color _____

Fruiting time and yield _____

Pests or diseases _____

• • •

Common name _____

Botanical name _____

Christian symbolism _____

Where and when purchased _____

Date planted _____ Date seeds/cuttings started _____

Watering needs _____

Garden location_____

Bloom time and color _____

Fruiting time and yield _____

Pests or diseases _____

• • •

Common name _____

Botanical name _____

Christian symbolism _____

Where and when purchased _____

Date planted _____ Date seeds/cuttings started _____

Watering needs _____

Garden location_____

Bloom time and color _____

Fruiting time and yield _____

Pests or diseases _____

• • •

Common name _____

Botanical name _____

Christian symbolism _____

Where and when purchased _____

Date planted _____ Date seeds/cuttings started _____

Watering needs _____

Garden location_____

Bloom time and color _____

Fruiting time and yield _____

Pests or diseases _____

• • •

Common name _____

Botanical name _____

Christian symbolism _____

Where and when purchased _____

Date planted _____ Date seeds/cuttings started _____

Watering needs _____

Garden location_____

Bloom time and color _____

Fruiting time and yield _____

Pests or diseases _____

• • •

Common name _____

Botanical name _____

Christian symbolism _____

Where and when purchased _____

Date planted _____ Date seeds/cuttings started _____

Watering needs _____

Garden location_____

Bloom time and color _____

Fruiting time and yield _____

Pests or diseases _____

• • •

Common name _____

Botanical name _____

Christian symbolism _____

Where and when purchased _____

Date planted _____ Date seeds/cuttings started _____

Watering needs _____

Garden location_____

Bloom time and color _____

Fruiting time and yield _____

Pests or diseases _____

• • •

Common name _____

Botanical name _____

Christian symbolism _____

Where and when purchased _____

Date planted _____ Date seeds/cuttings started _____

Watering needs _____

Garden location_____

Bloom time and color _____

Fruiting time and yield _____

Pests or diseases _____

• • •

Common name _____

Botanical name _____

Christian symbolism _____

Where and when purchased _____

Date planted _____ Date seeds/cuttings started _____

Watering needs _____

Garden location_____

Bloom time and color _____

Fruiting time and yield _____

Pests or diseases _____

• • •

Common name _____

Botanical name _____

Christian symbolism _____

Where and when purchased _____

Date planted _____ Date seeds/cuttings started _____

Watering needs _____

Garden location_____

Bloom time and color _____

Fruiting time and yield _____

Pests or diseases _____

• • •

Common name _____

Botanical name _____

Christian symbolism _____

Where and when purchased _____

Date planted _____ Date seeds/cuttings started _____

Watering needs _____

Garden location_____

Bloom time and color _____

Fruiting time and yield _____

Pests or diseases _____

• • •

Common name _____

Botanical name _____

Christian symbolism _____

Where and when purchased _____

Date planted _____ Date seeds/cuttings started _____

Watering needs _____

Garden location_____

Bloom time and color _____

Fruiting time and yield _____

Pests or diseases _____

• • •

Common name _____

Botanical name _____

Christian symbolism _____

Where and when purchased _____

Date planted _____ Date seeds/cuttings started _____

Watering needs _____

Garden location_____

Bloom time and color _____

Fruiting time and yield _____

Pests or diseases _____

• • •

Common name _____

Botanical name _____

Christian symbolism _____

Where and when purchased _____

Date planted _____ Date seeds/cuttings started _____

Watering needs _____

Garden location_____

Bloom time and color _____

Fruiting time and yield _____

Pests or diseases _____

∙ ∙ ∙

Common name _____

Botanical name _____

Christian symbolism _____

Where and when purchased _____

Date planted _____ Date seeds/cuttings started _____

Watering needs _____

Garden location_____

Bloom time and color _____

Fruiting time and yield _____

Pests or diseases _____

∙ ∙ ∙

Common name _____

Botanical name _____

Christian symbolism _____

Where and when purchased _____

Date planted _____ Date seeds/cuttings started _____

Watering needs _____

Garden location_____

Bloom time and color _____

Fruiting time and yield _____

Pests or diseases _____

• • •

Common name _____

Botanical name _____

Christian symbolism _____

Where and when purchased _____

Date planted _____ Date seeds/cuttings started _____

Watering needs _____

Garden location_____

Bloom time and color _____

Fruiting time and yield _____

Pests or diseases _____

• • •

Common name _____

Botanical name _____

Christian symbolism _____

Where and when purchased _____

Date planted _____ Date seeds/cuttings started _____

Watering needs _____

Garden location_____

Bloom time and color _____

Fruiting time and yield _____

Pests or diseases _____

• • •

Common name _____

Botanical name _____

Christian symbolism _____

Where and when purchased _____

Date planted _____ Date seeds/cuttings started _____

Watering needs _____

Garden location _____

Bloom time and color _____

Fruiting time and yield _____

Pests or diseases _____

• • •

Common name _____

Botanical name _____

Christian symbolism _____

Where and when purchased _____

Date planted _____ Date seeds/cuttings started _____

Watering needs _____

Garden location _____

Bloom time and color _____

Fruiting time and yield _____

Pests or diseases _____

Plant Selection and History

• • •

Common name _____

Botanical name _____

Christian symbolism _____

Where and when purchased _____

Date planted _____ Date seeds/cuttings started _____

Watering needs _____

Garden location_____

Bloom time and color _____

Fruiting time and yield _____

Pests or diseases _____

• • •

Common name _____

Botanical name _____

Christian symbolism _____

Where and when purchased _____

Date planted _____ Date seeds/cuttings started _____

Watering needs _____

Garden location_____

Bloom time and color _____

Fruiting time and yield _____

Pests or diseases _____

• • •

Common name _____

Botanical name _____

Christian symbolism _____

Where and when purchased _____

Date planted _____ Date seeds/cuttings started _____

Watering needs _____

Garden location_____

Bloom time and color _____

Fruiting time and yield _____

Pests or diseases _____

• • •

Common name _____

Botanical name _____

Christian symbolism _____

Where and when purchased _____

Date planted _____ Date seeds/cuttings started _____

Watering needs _____

Garden location_____

Bloom time and color _____

Fruiting time and yield _____

Pests or diseases _____

25
Wish List

We all have desires for garden additions that must be budgeted for, things like statues or icons, bird baths and feeders, outdoor furniture, tools, or that unique tree or shrub. When someone asks what you want as a gift, share from your list!

In Unit 1, chapter 4, you gathered ideas for items to be placed in the garden. Here you can catalog what items you want to purchase to track your budget in creating your prayer garden — whether for a public garden or a personal one — or enter what you need to budget for in the future

Wish List

Item	Budget/cost	Date acquired

Item	Budget/cost	Date acquired

About the Author

Margaret Rose Realy, Obl. OSB lives an eremitic life and is an award-winning author and freelance writer. She has a master's degree from Michigan State University, is an Advanced Master Gardener and certified greenhouse grower, and worked/volunteered in the green industry for over fifty-five years. She has been writing since 2007.

Margaret taught workshops at Michigan State University; she has written for the Diocese of Lansing, Patheos.com, *Jackson Citizen Patriot*, Catholic Digest, CatholicMom.com, Aleteia.com, and a column for OSV News called *The Catholic Gardener*.

Her previous book, *A Garden Catechism: 100 Plants in the Christian Tradition and How to Grow Them* won Association of Catholic Publishers 2023 Excellence in Publishing Award, 2nd Place, and took first place with Catholic Media Association for design. Her other books are *A Catholic Gardener's Spiritual Almanac; A Garden of Visible Prayer: Creating a Personal Sacred Space One Step at a Time;* and *Cultivating God's Garden through Lent*.

Create Your Own Index

A

B

C

D

E

F

G

H

I

J

K

L

M

N

O

P

Q

R

Create Your Own Index

S

T

U

V

W

X

Y

Z